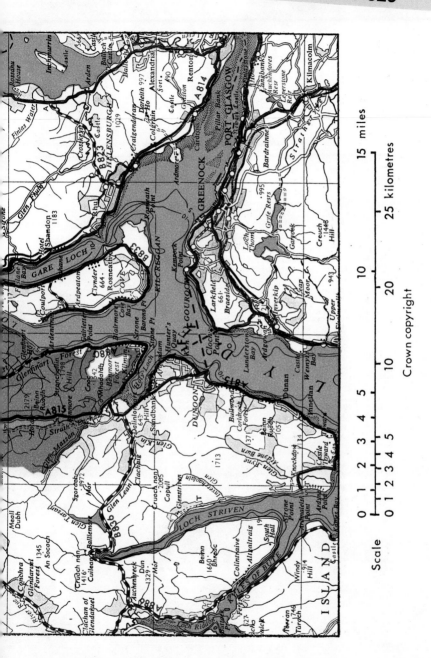

Scale

0 1 2 3 4 5 miles

0 1 2 3 4 5 10 20 kilometres

Crown copyright

ARGYLL
FOREST PARK

Beside Loch Eck

FORESTRY COMMISSION GUIDE

ARGYLL
FOREST PARK

Edited by
HERBERT L. EDLIN, BSc, DipFor
Forestry Commission

EDINBURGH
HER MAJESTY'S STATIONERY OFFICE

First published 1939
Fifth edition 1976

ISBN 0 11 710129 X

CONTENTS

v

ACKNOWLEDGEMENTS

IN addition to the contributors whose names appear on the title page, and the poets whose names are appended after each verse, the following people gave valued assistance with the production of this guide.

Mr. D. A. Mithen, formerly Conservator of Forests for West Scotland and now Director of Forest Management, and his staff. In particular Mr. Roger Hurst, Conservation and Recreation Officer for the West Conservancy, advised on editing and illustration.

Art Work The cover picture, chapter headings and in-text drawings are the work of Colin Gibson, D.A., of Monifieth.

The frontispiece is by David Walker.

Cartography The topographical maps have been prepared by John Watson, head of the Forestry Commission West Scotland Conservancy drawing office staff in Glasgow. They are based on the work of the Ordnance Survey, by permission of the Controller of Her Majesty's Stationery Office.

The geological map is adapted from the Geological Society.

Photographs The following photographers kindly contributed the under-noted pictures. Douglas Green, a Forestry Commission staff photographer, plates 1, 2, 14, 21, 23, 24, 27, 30, 47, 56 and 67. Herbert L. Edlin, plates 3, 4, 6, 8, 10, 16, 18, 66 and 68. Harry Watson, plate 5. C. Douglas Bolton, plates 7, 9 and 69. William L. Inglis, plates 11, 29, 55, 59 and 70. Messrs. Valentines of Dundee, plate 12. Robert M. Adam, plates 13, 20, 26 and 28, by permission of Messrs. D. C. Thomson, Dundee. Alastair Alpin MacGregor, plates 15 and 17. Hamish McInven, plates 19 and 25. George P. Simpson, of Greenock, plate 22. John Marchington, plates 31, 34 and 41. Don MacCaskill, plates 32, 33, 35, 36, 48, 52 and 61. Dr. H. D. Slack, plates 37, 38, 39, 40, 42, 43, 44, 45 and 46. Mrs. Hazel Geoffrey, a Forestry Commission staff photographer, plate 49. Tom Weir, plates 50 and 51. *The Scotsman* newspaper, plates 53 and 54. Carol Gibbs, plate 57. John Gillies, plate 58. B. H. Humble, plates 60, 62, 63, 64 and 65.

FOREWORD

BY THE SEVENTH EARL OF RADNOR, K.G., K.C.V.O.

CHAIRMAN OF THE FORESTRY COMMISSION, 1952–63

In 1935 the Forestry Commissioners set up a committee, under the Chairmanship of that great pioneer of Scottish forestry, Sir John Stirling-Maxwell, which advised them to create, amid the beautiful hills and lochs of the Cowal peninsula of Argyll, the first of Britain's Forest Parks. The guiding spirit in this movement was the late Lord Robinson of Kielder Forest and of Adelaide, who was at that time the Chairman of the Forestry Commission. In this, as in so many things, he showed himself to be thinking well ahead of the current trend, for the Argyll Forest Park was in existence ten years before the Dower Report advocated the formation of the larger National Parks in England and Wales. Today we have seven Forest Parks, five of them being in Scotland, which attract an ever-growing stream of visitors each year.

When the Argyll Forest Park was first formed most of its plantations were still in their infancy, and many stretches of the hillsides had yet to be planted up. In the thirty-one years that have elapsed the woods have grown greatly in stature, until today there is no finer expanse of highland forest scenery in Britain than that from Strone Point on the Firth of Clyde, up the shores of Loch Eck to Glenbranter, with the peaks of Beinn Mhor and Beinn Bheula towering above the green woods in the glens and the blue waters of the lochs.

But perhaps the greatest change that has come to this beautiful region is the return of the people to hills that—only forty years ago, knew only the occasional passing of a solitary shepherd or gamekeeper. The afforestation that began in 1921 has meant productive employment for considerable numbers of men and women—in its fine forests the Forestry Commission already has some 160 people at work, while others are employed by timber merchants. Forest communities have been established at Succoth, Glenbranter, Strachur and Glenfinart, where groups of new houses have been set up. A growing volume of timber is leaving these hills for the mines and industries of Central Scotland, and the paper pulp mill and great sawmill at Fort William.

Yet these developments have in no way impaired the attractions of the Forest Park. More and more people have come to enjoy the climbs to the high peaks, the rambles through the tall woodlands, and the attractions of the loch shores which the Park makes accessible to all. The public camping ground at Ardgartan has proved especially popular, with over 50,000 people visiting it in the course of a year, while many others who visit the Park stay at hotels or the several Youth Hostels nearby. This popular guide book, which was first prepared by Professor Walton in 1938, has once again sold out and required revision. It gives me great pleasure to introduce you to its pages and to welcome you to this magnificent region of the Scottish Highlands.

RADNOR

INTRODUCTION

By Professor John Walton

The Argyll Forest Park consists of large stretches of forest, mountain and moorland lying to the west of Loch Long in the northern portion of Strathclyde. It is divided into two main areas. The northern area consists of Ardgartan and Ardgoil and forms a wedge of mountains between Loch Goil and Loch Long: the rest of the boundary is formed by a line which runs north-east from Arrochar round by Loch Lomond to Coiregrogain, next round the northern slopes of Beinn Ime to Glen Kinglas, and then follows approximately the road to Rest-and-be-Thankful and so on to Lochgoilhead. The southern area is bounded on the east by Loch Long and Loch Goil. Its western part consists of the Ben More ridge of mountains extending from Benmore to near Strachur on Loch Fyne. Its north-eastern boundary lies roughly on a line from Carrick Castle on Loch Goil to Strachur.

The two areas are built up of a group of estates, one of which, Ardgoil, was presented to the Corporation of the City of Glasgow by Mr. T. Cameron Corbett in 1906 and transferred by them to the Forestry Commission in 1965; the others were acquired directly by the Forestry Commission. The first planting done by the Commission was in Glenbranter in 1922, and since then the Commission has afforested large areas.

1

In 1935 the Forestry Commission, under the chairmanship of Sir Roy Robinson (later Lord Robinson), conceived the idea of utilising the area as a Forest Park, and the Corporation of Glasgow consented to co-operate.

The total area of the estates is about 60,000 acres, of which broad strips round the coasts and below 1,000 feet in altitude, amounting to about 23,000 acres, have been afforested, leaving approximately 37,000 acres available for grazing and recreation.

Besides this rugged and magnificent stretch of Highland scenery, the beautiful Younger Botanic Garden formed by the late Mr. Harry G. Younger at the southern end of the Park offers in its finely laid-out beds and shrubberies added attractions for visitors from the cities. Mr. James Duncan, the previous owner of the estate, had planted many kinds of trees, including the avenue of stately sequoias which form the approach to the house. Mr. Younger had made notable additions to the gardens, and now many of the beautiful flowering shrubs raised in the Royal Botanic Gardens in Edinburgh are planted at Benmore, where they find a most congenial climate. To visit the Younger Garden towards the end of May, when the rhododendrons are in bloom (and there are about 200 different species), is an experience not easily forgotten. Not far from the Garden is Puck's Glen, a place of great natural charm.

Arrochar and Lochgoilhead and the road between them offer the easiest points of access to the northern area, while Arrochar may be approached by rail as well. One can get to Dunoon and Hunter's Quay by ferry and thence on to Benmore or the southern part of the Park. Buses link Dunoon with Benmore and Strachur, or Ardentinny. Spacious public parking places for cars have been provided near Ardgartan House, and elsewhere.

Once the Park has been reached there are easy walks for those who like fine views and fresh air. For more ambitious pedestrians the district will provide an inexhaustible variety of rambles. The mountains at Ardgartan, particularly The Cobbler (2,891 feet) provide a certain amount of rock climbing for the expert. For those who seek them there are the solitude and peace of the mountains, the joys of exploration of high corries and bens, and for others the delights of easier expeditions along the singularly interesting coast.

The Park has its interests large and small; the naturalist will find here in the most minute detail of meadow, rock or stream, enough for lengthy study. At the same time one need not be deeply versed in science to appreciate fully the natural beauty of the district—the trees, the flowers, the animal life, all to be seen in such wonderful surroundings.

Those who read this guide will realise that the Park not only

2

provides scope for recreation and amusement, but that it should be regarded even more as a place where the past history of the country is revealed by the configuration of the land, and one where the native plants and animals of Scotland may be seen at their best in their natural setting. Nor is the past alone of interest. Forestry is one of the coming ways in which the land in the Highlands may be restored, not only for timber production but also for the livelihood and life of the people.

Look down on landscape—it's the charm
of its being there infects us:
the silent buglike tractors, the farm
between windbreak pines, the familiar loch
where undoubted fish are rising—all gathered
into one ancestral plot, convenient, perfect.

—Tom Buchan.

. . . . a standing
stone, a druidic lingam standing for nothing
anyone knows about nowadays, a stony
finger, green with years, specific of an idea
which was no doubt straight, strong and complex
once, but is now obliterated . . . .

—Tom Buchan.

HISTORY AND ANTIQUITIES
By Mairi Paterson

A GLANCE at the map of Scotland will show that the Argyll Forest Park occupies the northern end of the Cowal Peninsula, that great three-pronged mass which seems to hang poised over the Island of Bute. The peninsula is bounded on the west by Loch Fyne and on the east by Loch Long, and while much of the area is remote and mountainous, these two great sea-lochs have been important routes since prehistoric times. Their fertile fringes and river valleys and straths such as Glendaruel and the valley of the River Cur seem to have attracted settlers since earliest times.

PREHISTORY

The tremendous mantle of ice which covered most of Britain during the Great Ice Ages meant that human occupation was

4

impossible. It was not until the ice began to retreat that vegetation could appear and animals come to browse upon it. The change was long and very gradual and it was not until about 5,000 B.C. that man first appeared in the West of Scotland. Mesolithic (Middle Stone Age) hunters and food gatherers came north, following the herds of wild animals, and established summer camps along the coastline. They did not settle here but retreated further south during the harsh winters. By about 3,000 B.C. they were forming more permanent settlements, notably near Oban, on the little island of Risga in Loch Sunart and at other places on the sea coast of Argyll, leaving their middens (great heaps of shells) as proof of their presence.

Among our earliest settlers were the first of the Neolithic farmers. They established themselves in south-west Scotland about 3,000 B.C. and gradually penetrated further north. Their culture, based on farming, rather than hunting and food-gathering, had taken over 2,000 years to reach Britain from its beginnings in the Near East.

Farming methods were effective but wasteful, and this led to the continual movement of people which characterises this period. Ground was cleared for farming by what is known as the "slash and burn" technique, and small plots of corn and barley cultivated. As ground became exhausted and unproductive, new areas were cleared and brought under cultivation. Cattle, sheep, pigs and goats were kept. We know very little of their settlements, because huts would be made of wood and turf, which disappear completely. Within recent years, however, an important Neolithic living site has been excavated in Glendaruel. This gave evidence of two distinct periods of occupation. Finely worked flint tools and sherds of pottery were found on this site, but the only traces of huts were their blackened hearths. If their houses have vanished, firm evidence of the presence of these Neolithic peoples remains in their immense tombs. These were built of great slabs of stones (megaliths), sometimes with an impressive forecourt, and with the hole covered with a huge cairn of stones. The cairn is in some cases over 100 feet long, covering a burial chamber which may be only 16 feet in length. During the thousands of years since their construction most of these "chambered cairns" have been robbed of their covering stones for road-making or dyke-building, but the great slabs of the burial chambers remain. These may be seen very clearly at Adam's Grave, near Sandbank, and in the fine cairn at Ach-na-ha, near the Otter Ferry–Kilfinan road.

The next wave of incomers were the first metal-workers. Copper was the first metal used, but was soon improved by mixing it with tin to produce the alloy, bronze. These peoples came in a series of waves bringing slightly different tools, weapons and customs with them. They buried their dead singly (unlike the Neolithic peoples with their communal tombs), in small box-like stone "cists" which were then covered by a round cairn of stones and earth. One of the most important centres in the British Isles of these bronze-using peoples was at Kilmartin, near Lochgilphead, so it is not surprising that their influence is found in Cowal on the opposite shore of Loch Fyne. There are a number of round cairns near Kilfinan, and several at Portavadie. Bronze Age people left other mysterious evidence of their presence—single or grouped standing stones and boulders or rock faces covered with cup marks, whose purpose or meaning is quite unknown. There is a very fine standing stone at Stillaig, near Portavadie and another at Fearnoch, near Kilfinan.

On the Continent, the use of iron, first discovered in the Near East, was becoming universal. A constant stream of immigrants brought these new ideas and techniques into Scotland, and by about 200 B.C. the use of iron was general. This new way of life was a war-like one, typified by the Celtic-speaking peoples, who had spread, from their original homelands in Austria and Switzerland, over most of the mainland of Europe and into Britain and Ireland. A later wave of these Celtic warriors crossed to Argyll from Northern Ireland, bringing with them their language, customs and rich, barbaric culture. Their language survives in Gaelic, spoken until comparatively recently in Cowal, and still evident in the place names of the peninsula. Their culture with its rich elaboration of design can be seen in the crosses and grave-slabs which are in the Lamont Vault at Kilfinan Church and on the fine mediaeval carved stones in the lapidarium in Kilmodan Churchyard, Glendaruel. It also survives in many of the Celtic souvenirs offered to tourists. Their customs—in particular their delight in warfare—have left us the many hill forts, duns and defended sites which mark this area. Some of the most notable of these are the magnificent Barr Iola, near Otter Ferry, Barmore, at the entrance to Glendaruel, and Inverglen near Strachur. The last of these is particularly interesting as it is really two forts, one within the other, of different periods. There are many others within the bounds of the Forest Park itself, and at times it appears that almost every prominent knoll had been fortified.

CELTIC MISSIONARIES AND VIKING RAIDERS

While it is possible that Christianity first came to Cowal with St. Ninian's missionaries from Whithorn in Galloway, there is as yet no definite evidence of this. Celtic monks, however, from St. Columba's great monastery at Iona came to Cowal to establish chapels in many places. Some of these have completely disappeared, leaving evidence of their presence only in place names with the

6

prefix "kil" (from *cill*—a chapel) as in Kilbride near Dunoon, and Kilfinan. Others may lie beneath or have been incorporated into the later mediaeval churches, as seems to have happened at Strachur, where the present church lies within a circular enclosure which is typical of the early Celtic Church, and at Kilmun, where there has been a series of ecclesiastical buildings. Kilmodan, in Glendaruel, has a number of early grave-stones which are well worth visiting. The Church of the Three Brethren at Lochgoilhead is a most interesting building and its dedication suggests that the site is a very early one. Recent excavations at Ardnadam beside Loch Loskin have revealed the walls of an early chapel with around it a complex of foundations of huts and other structures of different periods, indicating a lengthy occupation of this site.

As yet no definitely Norse settlements have been found, although there is no doubt that Viking longships cruised up the sea lochs. In 1110 a battle took place in Glendaruel between the Scots and invading Norsemen, and in 1263 a Norse fleet anchored off Arrochar, some of the boats were dragged across the isthmus to Tarbet on Loch Lomond and the Vikings harried the shores and islands of the Loch.

THE CLAN PERIOD

During the early clan period the dominant families appear to have been the Lamonts, the MacLachlans, the MacNaughtons and the MacEwans. By the fourteenth century, however, the powerful Campbell clan had acquired much of the land and their influence and power gradually extended to most of Cowal. Many of the castles, some in ruins, a few occupied and many now only names on the map, date from this troubled period of clan warfare. Castle Lachlan is an impressive ruin on the shore of Loch Fyne, and Toward Castle, seat of the Lamonts, is at present being excavated and restored. Knockamillie Castle, a Campbell stronghold behind Innellan, has only one wall standing, while MacEwan's Castle, on Loch Fyne, was only a name on the map and some uneven ground until its excavation some years ago. The site of the Castle at Dunoon is a very commanding one and there is no doubt that this was one of the earliest stone castles in Argyll. Unfortunately very little of its fabric has survived centuries of neglect. One of the most impressive castles in this area is the great Keep at Carrick on Loch Goil. This dates from the 15th century and stands on a rock by the shore, just beside the boundary of the Argyll Forest Park.

During the 17th century Cowal figured prominently in two dramatic incidents. In 1646 the long feud between the Campbells and the Lamonts reached its climax in the sacking and destruction

7

of the two Lamont castles at Toward and Ascog (near Portavadie). The Lamont leaders were hanged at Dunoon. This tragic event is commemorated by the Lamont Memorial in Dunoon. The Memorial Stone is situated on the little Tom-a-mhoid—the Hill of Judgment. In 1685 the ninth Earl of Argyll brought a small force from Holland to invade Scotland in an attempt to aid Monmouth's rising in the West of England against James VII and II. Argyll's small army landed at Loch Riddon and after several local skirmishes marched along the shore of Loch Eck and crossed over the Larach to Ardentinny from where they crossed to Coulport by boat. The ill-fated expedition met its end in Dunbartonshire and Argyll himself was captured at Inchinnan. He was later tried and beheaded in Edinburgh. It is from this period that the story of the "Paper Cave" dates. Savage reprisals followed Argyll's abortive rising and local tradition states that valuable documents belonging to the Argyll family were concealed in a cave on the slopes of Ben More, near Coirantee on Loch Eck.

By this time travel in Cowal depended on the use of ferries and tracks over the saddles of hills, through passes or by lochsides. Ferries formerly crossed Loch Long at Whistlefield, near Portincaple, north of Garelochhead, to Carrick or Mark on the west side. Thence through routes ran up the shores of Loch Goil and over the hills to Strachur and St. Catherine's to link with another ferry across Loch Fyne to Inveraray. Other ferries crossed Loch Long from Gourock or Coulport to Ardentinny, whence the Larach road led to Whistlefield on Loch Eck. A further ferry across Loch Eck took the traveller westward by the Bernice Gap towards Loch Fyne, and still more ferries.

All this sounds complicated, but was actually much more direct than by modern roads, and about half as long. The Dukes of Argyll are said to have travelled to the Lowlands by the route Inveraray—ferry to St. Catherine's—Lochgoilhead—Mark—ferry to Portincaple. This route was both quick and direct, and had, in addition, the virtue of passing only through the lands of those friendly to Argyll.

CROFTERS AND CLEARANCES

Until the middle of the eighteenth century the area of the Forest Park consisted mainly of crofting settlements. A small group of houses constituted a " clachan " and usually the work and recreation was communal. The grazings on the hill were held in common and in the summer the young people of the clachan would move up on to the high pastures to live in the little huts or "sheilings". Recently a typical group of houses was re-discovered among the trees on the shores of Loch Eck, while on the open hillside above the tree line lay the well-preserved foundations of the sheilings, complete with a store house. Cattle were the main livestock, together with the hardy Highland ponies, while oats and barley were grown on the small strips of cultivated ground. Fishing was an essential part of this subsistence economy and Loch Fyne herring were a notable export to the South.

The cattle, described as small, black, sturdy beasts, were found all over the Highland area. In his book *The Drove Roads of Scotland*, A. R. Haldane describes the routes by which the animals were brought—on the hoof—to great markets like the Falkirk Tryst. Many of these routes from the North and from the Isles converged in Argyll and the tracks and passes of Cowal formed an important section of the route to the ferries at Ardentinny and Dunoon. Cattle from Islay, for example, were brought to the mainland, driven up to the southern end of Loch Awe and taken across to Loch Fyne by a track, which is now a public footpath. They were ferried across the loch and then driven over the Larach to Ardentinny or down the west side of Loch Eck and past Loch Loskin (where stretches of the old road can still be seen) to the ferry at Dunoon.

Although Argyll did not suffer the tragic "Clearances" when landowners evicted their tenants by force to make way for large sheep farms, a change in the use of the land was bound to take place. About 1750, the mysterious Thomas Harkness, known as *an Gall*

9

Ruadh (the red-haired stranger) appeared in Cowal, driving his sheep before him. He acquired the farm of Glenkin and became one of the most prosperous men in the district. He was merely the first of the new sheep farmers from the south who offered good rents for the grazings on the old croft lands. As the author of the description of Dunoon Parish wrote in the *First Statistical Account of Scotland (1791)*: "These southland shepherds have within 40 or 50 years, altered almost entirely the stock of the mountains—from black cattle and horses to sheep, by which they have raised the rents, all over this country, considerably, as well as enriched themselves."

EARLY FORESTRY

During this period, too, the natural woodland, mainly oak, birch and alder, on the lower hill slopes was being utilised. Oakwoods were coppiced on a regular twenty year rotation to yield poles and firewood as well as bark and charcoal. The bark was used for tanning leather and the wood was then turned into charcoal. This was essential for smelting the bog iron which was comparatively plentiful though not of high quality. This method of procuring iron for tools or weapons had been used for many centuries and was virtually unchanged from the techniques introduced by the first iron using peoples. Forestry ploughs have revealed many of these charcoal burning or iron smelting sites, easily recognisable by the quantities of charcoal or the unmistakable slag heaps.

By 1750, however, the Industrial Revolution had come to the Highlands and the great iron-smelting works at Furnace on Loch Fyne were in operation. Much of the native woodland of Argyll was felled to supply the great furnace which gave the village its name. While Cowal had no iron-smelting works on this scale, it did have a gunpowder factory at Millhouse, near Kames, and another in Glen Lean, near Dunoon. The ruins of the houses and of the widely separated gunpowder stores can still be seen, and it was only recently that the Cooperage at Sandbank was demolished. This was where the barrels to contain the gunpowder were made.

The felling of the natural timber on the hills led to the gradual impoverishment of the land. The regeneration of the trees was severely affected by the close cropping of the grazing sheep and the custom of burning to clear more ground. As the land became poorer Cheviot sheep (the breed first brought to the area by the southern farmers) gave way to the hardier and less demanding Blackface breed.

By the 1920's afforestation had begun to replace sheep farming in much of Cowal. As in earlier days the wood was used for industrial purposes, but both the wood and its uses had changed. The trees were mainly coniferous with occasional plantings of deciduous trees for amenity reasons. The forests are planted, cultivated and felled as a crop with the mature trees going to the saw mills and the thinnings being taken by lorry and train to the pulp mill at Fort William to be used in paper-making. This intense cultivation demands a continuous labour force, and has led to the creation of forestry villages such as Glenbranter, near Strachur, and the building of groups of forestry houses as at Arrochar, Glendaruel, and on Loch Eck side.

THE VICTORIAN PERIOD

Another change had been gradually taking place. For much of its history, Cowal had been regarded as remote from the lowlands and as a Gaelic-speaking crofting or farming area. During the Victorian period, however, all this began to change and Cowal developed closer links with the lowlands, and, in particular with the new industrial giant, Glasgow. This was largely due to the great increase of regular ferries and steamer services on the Firth of Clyde. It soon became practicable to travel to Glasgow to work, while living in a district of great scenic beauty unspoiled by industrialisation. The little Highland villages of Dunoon, Innellan and Blairmore were transformed by the fine villas of the Glasgow merchants, piers were built and roads improved. Wealthier businessmen bought estates and built grand mansions—it is from this period that such houses such as Castle Toward, Invereck, Dunselma at Strone, Drimsynie at Lochgoilhead, and Benmore, with its noted gardens, date. Many of these wealthy new landowners improved their land by creating gardens and by afforestation of the hill slopes. Since the decline of the wealthy families, much of this land has passed under the control of the Forestry Commission, and has indeed formed the nucleus of the Argyll Forest Park.

RECENT DEVELOPMENTS

Today the emphasis on holiday-making is changing, but the Park is playing its part in the new interest in the open air. It gives the holiday-maker the opportunity to enjoy some of the finest scenery in the country in freedom. The hills are open to the walker and naturalist while the rock climber can tackle hills like Ben Ime near the top of the Rest-and-be-Thankful road, and the famous Cobbler, near Arrochar. Forestry roads are open to walkers—though not to cars—and provide a network of paths with frequent magnificent views. Pony trekkers can ride on the forestry roads and are often seen near Strachur and at Lochgoilhead. At Lochgoilhead, too, is a large Boy Scout centre where hill walking, orienteering, sailing and canoeing instruction is given. At Benmore there is an Adventure

Centre for school children, which is run by Lothian Education Authority. The success of this type of outdoor training has recently been emphasized by the establishment of an Outdoor Education Centre at Ardentinny by the Education Department of the Region of Strathclyde, using the magnificent Glenfinart Forest for hill walking and climbing and Loch Long for sailing and canoeing.

The Commission has gone further than merely allowing those interested to use the natural facilities available in the Park. Within recent years a number of interesting Nature Trails have been established, several of them based on the Arboretum at Kilmun, where there are plantings of many unusual trees. Other trails have been planned on the hillside above Loch Riddon, near the fine new road to Tighnabruaich. Hides have been built and a picnic site laid out. The Commission has shown an enlightened attitude towards the history of the area by its willingness to report discoveries and to assist in leaving them available for expert study by archaeologists or historians.

As a result of this growing development of interest in open-air pursuits, the Commission has found it necessary to provide camping grounds and caravan sites. Sites such as Ardgartan are extremely popular as there is ready access to fine walking or climbing country. A series of booklets and maps give useful information and guidance.

History is too often thought to be a record of the more dramatic and exciting incidents of the past; to deal with the actions of the great rather than the lives of the humble. Man's need to use the land he lives on remains constant, however, and in Cowal the changing pattern of land use is a valuable record of social history. The land supported crops in the days of the Neolithic farmers, cattle and horses in the mediaeval and clan period, and sheep from 1750 until fifty years ago. Now trees cover the hillsides and the next chapter in our long history has begun.

I kept watch for a day in the treetops with thee,
I kept watch for two days in the sea wrack with thee,
I kept watch for a night on a sea rock with thee,
I kept watch, my love, and I did not regret it,
Wrapped in a corner of thy tartan plaid,
The spindthrift ever breaking over us,
Water that is very pure, cool, and wholesome.

—Seathan Mac Righ Eireann,
Seathan Son of the King of Ireland.

LEGENDS AND TRADITIONS
Contributed by Arthur Geddes,
Colin M. Macdonald and Herbert L. Edlin

THE GAEL IN COWAL AND STRATHCLYDE

When about 300–500 A.D., the Gael came from Ireland to western Scotland and gave that part lying between Loch Fyne and Loch Awe the name of Argyll, Tract of the Gael (*Earramh-Ghaedheal*), they brought with them a two-fold tradition. One side of it was their life in the wilds, with the chase, and the love of wood and mountain, stream and wave. No truer band of friends ever sailed these waters or ranged these glens than Deirdre, loveliest of women, her bridegroom Naoise*, and his two faithful brothers, Annle and Ardan. Deirdre, sought because of her surpassing beauty by Conchobar, King of Ulster, chose instead to fly to Scotland, there to range these hills with her beloved Naoise. In the end the three brothers returned with her to Ireland, at the King's behest. Three lovely stanzas of

---

* *The sound of 'e' in 'serve', or 'i' in 'mirth' may show how to pronounce the Scots Gaelic* ao, *as in* Naoise.

Deirdre's "Farewell to Alba" are now best known through the fine setting by Mrs. Kennedy-Fraser and Kenneth Macleod. Here is another stanza telling of how she who could have been a queen among white maidens, preferred to see the slender garlic in the oak woods of Argyll; and rather than be couched in a palace, to camp by Inver-Masan, with the restful but light sleep of one who lives in the wilds:

> "O Glen Masan, glen beloved,
>   Thy garlic's tall, the flower how white!
> Even-fall would bring us ease,
>   By grassy stream-mouth, sleeping light."

To leave Argyll brought Deirdre sorrow. You must read their story in the two exquisite versions written down by Carmichael in the Isle of Barra, seven hundred years after this song was written down in Glen Masan. Who composed the song? Surely it was Deirdre herself, centuries earlier still!

The second side of the traditions of life enjoyed by the Gael was that of the people labouring in common, linked by the brotherhood of work and play together, and blessed by a Christian faith still fresh from Galilee, still untouched by later doctrine. As in the Parables one can almost see Jesus afoot in Galilee, so in the hymns of the Gael, we hear and see the sounds and sights of creation stir about the saints who composed these hymns, and the people who remembered and sang them. We may remember lines from a hymn by Saint Patrick, composed at the crisis of his mission:

> "At Tara today in this fateful hour
> I place all Heaven with its power,
> And the sun with its brightness,
> And the snow with its whiteness . . .
> Fire . . . lightning . . . winds . . . sea . . . rocks . . .
> And the earth with its starkness:
>   All these I place,
> By God's almighty help and grace
> Between myself and the powers of darkness."

Here, where forester and farmer are together trying to make a part of the Highlands fruitful once more, a place where fellowship may build a new home, we should remember how the Gaelic people practised team-work. When the men ploughed, they pooled their pony-teams; and as they sailed, there were "Four to row and one to steer"—singing as they rowed. As the women went busily about their homes, tending them (they said) "as Mary did, in her day", they lit their fires at morn and covered them at eve, baked the bannocks, and wove the striped or the checked cloth, the tartan, with prayer. Prayer-poems such as you may be allowed—in deep

14

intimacy—to hear in the Outer Isles even today, were spoken, chanted and sung by Loch Long-side, not so very long ago. Best of all the collections (and translations) of these glorious prayers and hymns is that by Alexander Carmichael, which he called *Carmina Gadelica*. A fine volume, the third, was brought out by his grandson, who soon after, in 1941, left his university chair and joined the Navy—he had been a keen waterman on these lochs and rivers. He never returned, but he has left us great riches.

A. G.

THE OLD CELTIC PERIOD

This period was more remarkable for its ecclesiastical greatness than for its political achievements although its ceaseless efforts for territorial expansion were marked by numerous military successes and defeats, with the former predominating on the whole.

Iona symbolised all that was great in the religious life of old Celtic times; the influence of men of religion was paramount in all spheres but, outstandingly so, in their own calling. Columba is universally known for his missionary enterprises but his very prominence has tended to overshadow the work of other energetic Celtic missionaries whose efforts are becoming much better appreciated as impartial research progresses. Among these must be included Saint Mun from whom Kilmun on the Holy Loch derives its name. This saint, who, unfortunately, has far too often been confused with the celebrated saint of Glasgow, Saint Mungo or Kentigern, was a younger contemporary of Columba and is mentioned by Adamnan, the latter's biographer. He was an Irish-born Celtic saint who carried on his religious work not only in the area of the Holy Loch but also in the districts of Mid Argyll and Lorn where the Kilmuns near Inveraray and Loch Avich bear witness to his fame and influence. He appears to have penetrated to the shores of Appin and Loch Linnhe where the name of St. Munda's isle off Ballachulish still remains to record his memory. He is believed to have died about the year 635; his day of remembrance is 21 October.

C. M.

THE KINGDOM OF DALRIADA

The earliest records and traditions concerning the Forest Park lands begin with the arrival of Gaelic-speaking invaders from the north of Ireland. These people called themselves Scots, and their descendants, under King Kenneth Macalpin, eventually, in 843 A.D., overcame the Picts, and gave their name to the whole of Scotland. "Argyll", from *Earramh Ghaedhal*, means the "Coastland of the Gaels"; while "Dalriada" means the "Fields of Riada", and takes this name from the half-legendary Irish leader Caibre Riada, who is believed to have invaded mid-Argyll in 258 A.D. The centre of

15

his power was the fortress of Dunadd, which lies to the west of Cowal, near Lochgilphead.

About the year 498 there was a further colonisation of Argyll by other Irish Dalriadic Gaels, whose chieftains, the sons of Erc, were named Loarn, Angus and Fergus. Each of these leaders founded a tribe or clan. Lorne, the district around Oban, is named after the first of them and the county of Angus after the second. Comghall, a grandson of Fergus, gave his name to the Cowal Peninsula.

The heroic and romantic sides of such invasions were recorded in the Ossianic song poems, which have been translated from the Gaelic by Macpherson and others. They show clear links with Irish traditions, as revealed in ancient Irish manuscripts. One of the few authentic Scottish Gaelic records, the Glen Massan manuscript which tells of the wanderings of the princess Deirdre, was found in the house of a "forester"—probably a proprietor who held hunting rights, in Glen Massan beside Benmore forest. This manuscript is possibly of thirteenth century date and may have been transcribed by the monks of Kilmun; it is now preserved in the National Library of Scotland at Edinburgh.

Saint Columba, one of the earliest Christian missionaries, came to Dalriada from Ireland in the year 563. He founded the famous monastery on the island of Iona, off the coast of Mull, and so carried forward those Christian traditions, derived indirectly from the Roman Empire, that have flourished in Scotland ever since. Despite the sacking of Iona by Norse invaders, and the revival of paganism farther east during the Dark Ages, here in the West the light of the Christian faith has always burnt undimmed.

The priests of this early Celtic church established religious centres at St. Catherines, Strachur, Strathlachlan, Glendaruel, Ardnadam and Kilmun; this last name implies the "cell" or chapel of Saint Mun, and explains the name of the Holy Loch nearby. A monastery of some importance developed at Kilmun, and some ruins of this remain beside the modern parish church. It was associated with Paisley Abbey and it received, in 1240, an endowment of "three half-penny lands" from a Lamont chieftain. In 1442, Sir Duncan Campbell of Lochow, King's Lieutenant for Argyll, gave it a further endowment for a provost and seven perpetual chaplains or prebendaries.

THE NORSEMEN

Between 795 and 1263 A.D. the whole western seaboard of Scotland came under the influence and eventual overlordship of the Norse vikings. They came first to plunder, then to settle. From strongholds in the Shetland and Orkney Islands they conquered the Hebrides and set up colonies in Kintyre, Galloway, Ireland, the Isle of Man, north-west England and Yorkshire, leaving abundant place-names to record their settlement. But northern Cowal, lying off the main route south, and having a rugged terrain that was less fertile than neighbouring lands, does not appear to have attracted their main onslaught. Moreover, the Gaels of this region were sufficiently powerful to maintain their independence throughout.

The Park and its adjacent waters do not figure in the Norse sagas until the final chapter, in 1263 A.D. Then Haakon, king of Norway, who reigned at Bergen, came with a great war-fleet to Loch Long, which the Norsemen called *skipafjördr*, or the "firth of ships". He anchored near Arrochar, and some of his men actually dragged boats across the narrow isthmus to Tarbet. There they launched their craft on Loch Lomond, and made forays to its cultivated shores and islets. But during the same summer Haakon's army was defeated at the Battle of Largs by the Scottish king, Alexander. In 1266 the Norse kings finally relinquished all their claims to the Western Highlands and Islands, retaining only Orkney and Shetland.

H. L. E.

THE WARS OF INDEPENDENCE AND THE CLANS

If space allowed, one could tell many a stirring tale, for as Barbour wrote in his "Bruce"; "Ah! freedom is a noble thing!" You must read therein how Bruce crossed Loch Lomond as a fugitive from the Lowlands with Douglas and a few men—they had just been forced to part from the women they loved. Both ends of the loch were watched by Bruce's enemies, who had taken or hidden every boat. The faithful Sir Neil Campbell of Loch Awe had been sent ahead.

> " *The King, efter that he*[1] *was gane,*
> *To Loch Lomond the way has ta'en,*
> *And came there on the third day.*
> *But thereabout nae boat found they,*
> *That micht them ou'r the water bear . . .*
> *Sae busily they socht, and fast,*
> *Till James of Douglas, at the last,*
> *Found a little sunken boat,*
> *And to the land it drew, full hot*[2].
> *But it so little was that it*
> *Micht ou'r the water but threesome*[3] *flit.*
> *But some of them could swim full weel*
> *And on his back bear a* fardele[4].
> *Sae, with swim-ming and with row-ing*
> *They brocht them ou'r, and all their thing.*
> *The king, the whilis, merrily,*
> *Read, to them what were him by,*
> *Romance of worthy Ferembrace . . ."*

---

[1] *i.e. Campbell*   [2] *quickly, hot-foot*
[3] *carry only three at a time*   [4] *a burden, Fr. fardeau*

17

Once all were safely across, they could make for Loch Long-head, and so over the passes to Loch Fyne and Loch Awe. But could there be a finer scene than this of the defeated Scots, their enemies massed at Balloch and Ardlui, their little band rowed two at a time across the loch for a day and a night, or swimming it with their rucksacks on their backs—and Bruce keeping hearts high by reading a romance of a worthy knight of Charlemagne? No wonder that the Scots, victorious at last, chose and crowned Bruce, King of Scots!

Wallace, too, was in the countryside of Lennox (Lomond and Leven-side, usually with Loch Long-head). As Blind Harry the Minstrel sang, of a time when Wallace sought refuge there:

> " *That land is strait, and maisterful to win,*
> *Gude men of arms that time was it within,*
> *The Lord was traist,* the men secure and true . . .* "

Did space allow, one would gladly re-tell clan tales, of the Colquhouns, MacFarlanes, MacArthurs, MacGregors, Lamonts and Campbells. Many of them are wild; but too much can be made of "clan devilry"!

What the hill-walker in Cowal is well-placed to understand is this. Most of the Highlanders or Gael, whose homes and lands were linked to the Firth of Clyde by loch and pass, were linked to Scottish unity. Of such were the Campbells through history, down from Colin Mor and his son Sir Neil MacChailin Mor who helped Bruce, with their castles on Loch Awe and Loch Fyne, and later, their foothold and burial place at Kilmun on Holy Loch, opposite the Lowlands. Other Gaels, more distant, felt the need for Gaelic independence, as did Clan Donald and the Lords of the Isles. Hence the long struggle of the chiefs of Clan Campbell against the chiefs of Clan Donald.

In spite of much suffering—fundamentally due to food shortage—the daily life of clanship of chiefs and clansfolk had many redeeming features. Above everything else was the bond uniting the clansfolk themselves, in work and play, in Christian faith and in pagan lore of the wilds, in sorrow and joy. They laboured out on the loch and in the glens: but in summer some sought the high pastures, the men in the belted plaid, or *breacan*, the women in the *arasaid*, light and warm. There they camped in the sheilings (of which you may still find the ruins) and herded and milked the kine, singing as they milked, the young ones courting as they sang!

A. G.

CLANS AND NOBLE FAMILIES

Political power in Argyll passed by degrees to the leading clans who each claimed a particular territory. The southern shores of Loch Fyne, close to the Forest Park, were occupied by the Maclachlans

* *Traist: trusty*

18

of Strathlachan, whose leaders were of Norse descent, Lochlan being Gaelic for Scandinavia. The eastern part of Ardgartan Forest lay in the domains of the Colquhouns of Luss, the leading clan on Loch Lomondside. Glenbranter and Loch Eck came first under the dominion of the Lamonts, then under the Campbells of Loch Awe, and their numerous descendants.

Gradually the Campbells of Loch Awe, whose stronghold of Inveraray Castle stands just across Loch Fyne from the Forest Park, assumed the political overlordship of most of Argyll. Cowal was thus linked with their stormy fortunes in the main stream of Scottish history, which began with their loyal support of Robert the Bruce against the English in the Edwardian war from 1300 to 1314 (Bannockburn). Subsidiary castles of the Campbells stood at Ardkinglas, Strachur on Loch Fyne, and at Carrick on Loch Goil; and there is a Campbell burial vault on the hillside at Kilmun, behind the modern church above the Holy Loch.

At one time or another most of the Forest Park lands were held by one branch or another of this great clan Campbell, who trace their descent from Sir Gillespie or Archibald Cambel of Menstrie (Clackmannanshire) first recorded in 1263. His son Sir Colin Cambel, "Calein Mor", of Lochawe, about the year 1296, was killed in a battle with the MacDougalls of Lorne. In the thirteenth century they acquired Innis-nan-Ruisk in the present Forest Park, and in the fourteenth century George Campbell of Loudoun (Ayrshire) held lands at Loch Goil.

Records of the Campbells Cowal holdings, given in Harvey-Johnstone's *Heraldry of the Campbells* (Johnston, Edinburgh, 1881) include the following:

House of Ardkinglas:

Archibald Campbell, First of Innellan and Captain of Dunoon, died *circa* 1589.

Donald, one of his sons, held Glen Massan, much of which lies in *Benmore Forest.*

Colin Campbell of Ardentinny (*Glenfinart, Benmore Forest*), died 1510.

Robert Campbell, Constable of Carrick (*Loch Goil, Ardgartan Forest*), *circa* 1513.

Archibald Campbell of Drumsynie (*Loch Goil, Ardgartan Forest*), *circa* 1583.

House of Strachur

Duncan Campbell of Strachur (beside *Glenbranter Forest*), died *circa* 1280.

Charles Campbell of Ballochyle (beside *Benmore Forest*), *circa* 1658.

19

The office of "deer forester" of the Forest of Benmore was habitually given by the head of the Campbell clan to one of the younger members of the proprietors in Cowal.

The Campbells waged a long feud with the Lamonts, whom they drove southwards from the Forest Park lands into the south of Cowal. In 1646, the Marquis of Argyll, who was also the eighth Earl, sacked the Lamont stronghold of Castle Toward, and hanged many of the Lamont leaders at Dunoon. But in 1661 this same Marquis became involved in political intrigues arising from his earlier co-operation with the Cromwellian government, and his support of the Scottish Covenanters against King Charles II. He was tried for high treason and beheaded at Edinburgh.

SOME ANCIENT BUILDINGS

Buildings or sites of mediaeval date are recorded at the following points in or near the Park:

Carrick Castle, on Loch Goil, an ancient stronghold of the Earl of Argyll, said to stand on the site of a Norse fortress.

Ardkinglas Castle, near St. Catherines.

Castle Lachlan, on Loch Fyne.

Dunderave Castle, on north shore of Loch Fyne.

Mill of Driep, near Glenbranter.

Dunoon Castle—now in ruins, but a strategic stronghold from the thirteenth to the seventeenth century.

Ruined crofts in Glen More, near Lochgoilhead.

The military road over the Rest-and-be-Thankful Pass was built by the 22nd Regiment and later repaired by General Wade.

H. L. E.

THE CAMPBELLS: DUNCAN AND HIS GRANDSON

The Campbells, whose leading family of Lochawe was favoured with having from early times notable chiefs, have a unique record in Argyll, Scottish and British history for more than seven centuries; they were at first knights, then earls and ultimately dukes. They acquired a footing in Cowal early in the fourteenth century when lands at Innis-nan-ruisk, still within the Forest Park, were gifted to them by a laird of the Menteith family.

Thereafter their gains of Cowal territory were rapid. In 1430 they came into possession of additional estates, now also forming part of the Forest Park, when George Campbell of Loudon in Ayrshire resigned to his kinsman Duncan of Lochawe all his rights to lands in the parish of Loch Goil. This, he stated, was on account of Duncan's friendship to him as "chief of all his kin and surname". Duncan was a remarkable man for proved ability and striking achievements; he was fittingly known by his Gaelic nickname of *anadh*, meaning "the fortunate". He was the first of his family to be spoken of as "Lord Campbell" by virtue of his status as a lord of the contemporary Parliament of Scotland. He was, moreover, the grandfather of a no less gifted Campbell than himself in the person of Colin, Chancellor of Scotland and the earliest to hold the Earldom of Argyll.

Duncan had his chief residence at Inveraray but he also had other mansions in Argyll including one that fell within the limits of the Forest Park, for it is on record that he granted from his "manor" of Stratheck in 1429 a deed of gift in favour of the Friar Preachers of Glasgow. This showed his practical interest in men of religion and was by no means an isolated act but merely the prelude to a more munificent benefaction when he founded and endowed in 1442 a collegiate or residential church at Kilmun; the purposes of the gift are incorporated in his charter and were, among other things, "for the glory of God, of St. Mun and all the saints". This serves to confirm the belief, based on evidence of the thirteenth century, that the church originally organised by St. Mun himself had not perished utterly but had survived the stormy times of Norse aggression.

Duncan gave the final proof of his lasting affection for Kilmun when he chose the church there as the place of burial for himself and his kinsfolk; and the recumbent statues of *Anadh* and of his wife beside him can still be seen within the Argyll Mausoleum to the present day.

Colin, whose father Celestine or Archibald or Gillespie, as he was sometimes known by alternative equivalents, died before succeeding to the headship of the Campbells, was at least the equal of his predecessor in ability and energy. In his lifetime the family fortunes continued to mount higher and ever higher. He became the Master of the King's Household and finally attained the highest national office when he was chosen Chancellor of Scotland. He also held the chief administrative and judicial posts within the county and acted for a time as royal "coroner" for the whole of Cowal. He was well rewarded for his valuable national and local services and did not forget or overlook, in the midst of his own advancement, the claims or hopes of his home territories. He secured by his own personal efforts the establishment at Inveraray in 1474 of the first Chartered Burgh in Argyll and followed up this success with another of a similar kind sixteen years later when Kilmun was granted in 1490 a charter of burghhood; its terms are highly interesting to us.

KILMUN: A BURGH OF BARONY

It was to be a free burgh of barony "for ever" with rights to buy and sell and to allow butchers, bakers and brewers to carry on their different trades. Its inhabitants were to have the right to elect bailies and other officials, to hold markets weekly and two fairs annually as well as to set up a market cross.

By one of the strange accidents or, perhaps ironies of history, Kilmun never functioned actively or vigorously as a burgh, as it might have done if the Lochawe Campbells had erected their principal castle in or near Kilmun and made it the equal or rival of their headquarters at Inveraray. They preferred that it should provide a peaceful burial-place for themselves and kindred Campbells rather than be their base for warlike or expansionist enterprises. The pressing demands of high national offices also interfered with the Campbells' opportunities for the development of burghal undertakings and so Kilmun languished as a burgh and finally died. Thus, it is a complete mistake to quote, as has sometimes been done, the names of perhaps a score of "Provosts" of Kilmun as a seemingly obvious proof of lengthy civic existence. The name of Provost, so far as Kilmun was concerned, was purely an ecclesiastical title, still in use in Scotland chiefly in Episcopalian or Roman Catholic church circles.

THE CROSIER OF SAINT MUN

Before the end of the fifteenth century, Earl Colin's successor, another Archibald, who later fell at Flodden Field in 1513, acquired by purchase in 1497 from John Colquhoun of Luss the lands of

22

Inverchapel, of Glenfinart and of Coylet, together with a half markland in the territory of Inverchapel "occupied by a certain procurator, or custodian, of the staff of Saint Mun, called in the Gaelic vernacular *deowray*". This is profoundly interesting to antiquaries and others to whom things of the past appeal. Sacred relics have at all times been of the greatest importance both on religious and on secular grounds to the devout. Nothing could exceed in significance the pastoral staff of saints or bishops, for the staff or crosier, as it was usually termed, served to maintain either in its original self or through later consecrated replicas, the link with its first possessor and subsequent successors down the ages. Thus we find reverential deference paid to the crosier of Saint Fillan in Perthshire and to the pastoral staff of Saint Moluag of Lismore in Argyll.

THE SIXTEENTH CENTURY CAMPBELLS

In this century the Campbell success reached a new peak. The third Earl, another Colin, known among Gaels as *meallach* or "lumpy-brow" because of his habitual frown, was selected by James V as the only Scottish military commander competent to deal with the rebellious Angus faction; he was richly rewarded for his services by the grateful king.

His successors, the fourth and the fifth Earls, were both named Archibald but were easily differentiated by their respective nick-names of *roy* meaning "red-haired" and of *don* standing for our "brown-haired". Both were conspicuous among the Protestant leaders in Reformation times and their resources in money and men were decisive at critical moments. The younger Archibald was highly influential at the Court of the young Scottish Queen Mary; he was the husband of her older half-sister, one of James V's natural daughters, but the marriage proved a tragic failure and ended in divorce.

Shortly after the Queen had left France for ever, she paid in 1563 a state visit to Inveraray, accompanied by a retinue of select Scottish nobles, including her host Earl Archibald in whose honour Mary and her escorting ladies wore gay costumes of tartan. Her half-brother Moray, afterwards Regent, the formidable James Douglas of Morton, her versatile secretary Maitland of Lethington, and numerous others were also in attendance on their Queen. On her return journey to her capital in Edinburgh she travelled through much of the territory now included in the Forest Park. She crossed Loch Fyne by ferry to Creggans at Strachur and made a stay overnight at Dreip House, near Glenbranter, at the head of Loch Eck.

Here she was the centre of an interesting ceremony when, at ten in the morning of July 27, Charles Campbell, the laird of Strachur, handed over "on bended knee" the charter to his lands and received thereafter a new grant for his estates.

It was later in this same century that an incident occurred, within the confines of the present Forest Park, that sheds a vivid light on the reactions of the Campbells if they thought that they had been wronged or insulted.

Colin Campbell, the sixth Earl, was of equal national importance with the two preceding Archibalds and rose to hold the Chancellorship of Scotland; he, like so many Campbell earls, had a nickname; his was *Teach* because his mother belonged to the Menteith family. After he succeeded to the Earldom in 1572 he was immersed in all the contemporary affairs of state. He quarrelled bitterly with Douglas of Morton who had succeeded to the Regency as the strong man required for a troubled country. Morton made in the course of his administration many enemies and in some cases deservedly so.

Earl Colin had chosen as his wife the widow of the murdered Moray, who had been given valuable Crown jewels to recompense him for advances made out of his private means for public purposes. His widow, on her marriage with Earl Colin, had retained the coveted jewels. Morton called upon the Countess to hand over the jewels as being Crown property but she refused and her husband stoutly supported her. A lengthy wrangle ensued in which the English Queen Elizabeth took part, but finally Earl Colin acting for his wife was compelled to hand over the jewels to the Court officials with much publicity and under circumstances which he felt were humiliating.

He retired from Edinburgh to mountainous Argyll where he was secure and refused to obey any commands of Morton. The latter in the course of his duties had occasion to send a message in writing to be delivered in person to the Earl. The messenger, one of the sacronsanct state heralds, did not find him at home in Inveraray so he proceeded to search for him and came upon him while he was hunting in the forest near Loch Eck. He tried to thrust the paper message into the Earl's hand but the latter would not accept it and pushed roughly past the herald on horseback. The Campbell attendants then came into action; they seized the luckless herald, put a halter round his neck and threatened to hang him forthwith unless he promised never to show face in Argyll again! The Regent was greatly enraged at the treatment undergone by his herald but could inflict no effective penalties on Earl Colin, who had the grim satisfaction several years later of concurring in Morton's execution by the guillotine on a doubtful charge of high treason.

THE SEVENTEENTH CENTURY CAMPBELLS

From the early days that had followed the emergence of the Lochawe Campbells into national and county prominence their

Plate 1. Children play on a sunny beach beside Loch Eck, deep in Benmore Forest north of Dunoon.

Plate 2. Walkers on a forest trail near Puck's Glen in Benmore Forest.

Plate 3. The car-ferry across the Clyde from Cloch Point nears the landing stage at Hunter's Quay.

Plate 4. Strone Point and Benmore Forest seen from the Dunoon ferry.

Plate 5. Loch Long at Blairmore, looking north.

Plate 6. On the high road from Dunoon towards Kilmun and Loch Eck.

Plate 7. Northward view up Loch Long from Arddarroch on the eastern shore. Ardgartan Forest rises on the left, up the rugged heights of "Argylls' Bowling Green".

Plate 8. View south from Arrochar across Loch Long towards Ardgartan Forest and The Brack.

Plate 9. Northward prospect from Sandbank near Dunoon across the Holy Loch towards Kilmun, Kilmun Arboretum (*left*) and Benmore Forest.

Plate 10. Ardgartan camping ground, with the warden's office and shelter hut. The Cobbler rises beyond.

Plate 11. Kilmun Kirk, the traditional burial place of the Dukes of Argyll.

Plate 12. Carrick Castle beside Loch Goil.

Plate 13. Benmore House, now an Outdoor Training Centre for Lothian school-children.

Plate 14. The roadside monument at Glenbranter, erected by Sir Harry Lauder in memory of his son, Captain John Lauder, who fell in the 1914–1918 war.

Plate 15. Westward view from Lochgoilhead, across Loch Goil towards Beinn Bheula.

Plate 16. Loch Long and "Argyll's Bowling Green", seen from Craggan on the eastern shore, with Coilessan Glen running inland below The Brack.

career of success and of almost magical good fortune had been so undimmed that they seemed to be wholly immune from the hazards of human fate and from the winds of misfortune. But a revolutionary change was witnessed in the seventeenth century and they were almost completely overwhelmed by crushing disaster. The eighth Earl, who was the first and only Campbell Marquis, and his son and successor, the ninth in the line of Earls, both perished by the axe after trials that were unquestionably travesties of justice and legality. The Marquis, though by no means a saint himself in his dealings with Highlanders, was beheaded in 1661 for his "treasonable" co-operation with the Cromwellian government and for his acquiescence in the destruction of the "Martyr King", Charles I. His son suffered the same fate about twenty-four years later for his share in the futile and fatal Protestant insurrections in England and in Scotland led by the Duke of Monmouth against the fanatical Roman Catholic monarch, James II. The huge Campbell estates were forfeited, after being subjected to the indignities of invasion and occupation by the Athollmen. Even the very name of Campbell was marked out for extinction as had happened earlier in the century to the less lucky MacGregors. Fortunately, however, the timely overthrow of the despotic King, James II, saved the clan and their rulers from destruction. Thereafter, phoenix-like, they rose from their ashes and started afresh on a notable career of national and county public service.

THE JACOBITE PERIOD

With the "glorious Revolution" of 1688, it seemed that the Stuart rulers of Britain had come to a deserved end but they did not readily submit to their downfall and made at least three attempts at restoration. The "Fifteen" was crushed after the victory of John, the second Duke of Argyll, a "Marlborough" man, at Sheriffmuir. The uprising of 1719 was a sheer fiasco from the outset, but the "Forty-five" was more dangerous until the battle of Culloden was fought. The third, fourth and fifth Dukes of Argyll, with the overwhelming majority of their adherents throughout all parts of the county, supported the cause of the Hanoverians who were deeply in their debt for services rendered. One exception to the general Campbell loyalty was Colin, the laird of Glendaruel; his estate was forfeited. It is now, after numerous subsequent changes of ownership, included in part within the area of the Commission's Forests.

C. M. M.

COUNTRY ESTATES AND SEASIDE VILLAS

During the Victorian era, the disappearance of the crofters, the rise of the sheep grazings, and the general improvement of trade

25

and communications, made northern Cowal an attractive district for wealthy industrialists who wished to set up country estates and build large mansion houses. It was from such estates that the lands forming the modern forests were acquired. The experience of their owners, in planting many kinds of introduced trees, has proved of considerable value to modern foresters. In detail, the main acquisitions from large estates have been these:

Ardgartan Forest
> Largely from the Ardgartan Estate. Mansion now demolished.

Loch Goilhead portions of Ardgartan Forest
> Partly from the Ardgoil Estate of Mr. R. Cameron Corbett, partly from Drumsynie Estate. Drumsynie House is now a hotel.

Glenbranter Forest
> From Glenbranter Estate, once owned by Sir Harry Lauder. The mansion has been demolished.

Benmore Forest
> From the Benmore Estate of Mr. Harry G. Younger. The mansion is now an outdoor educational centre and the grounds have become a botanic garden.

Glenfinart portion of Benmore Forest
> From Glenfinart Estate once owned by the Earls Dunmore and the Douglas family. The mansion was burnt down several years ago.

At the same time the development of regular ferries and steamer services across and along the Clyde brought to the district a new kind of resident—the holiday-maker, retired business man, or city worker who found he could easily keep in touch with Glasgow and its neighbourhood from this attractive Highland fringe. Dunoon developed rapidly into a seaside resort, and a string of villas, each with its view of the sea, came into being along the shores of the Holy Loch. Lochgoilhead, which once had its own steamers, likewise developed. All this made the Forest Park more accessible, but did not alter its essentially attractive character of mountain, forest and loch.

H. L. E.

When Deirdre brought her sorrow
she won the sea birds native of this isle
with her brave lament
for still they cry her elegy
along these sacred shores.

You became the welcome one
of scheming gulls
who sent their shadows
climbing the lime-stone cliffs
aloof and dedicated
in the viking wind.
                                    —Charles Senior.

. . . Stand with us here.
Feel underfoot the linked vertebrae of your land
Standing north to the far fells, the heads of rivers.
Prehistory sleeps below in many beds.
    —Cecil Day Lewis, *Noah and the Waters.*

GEOLOGY

By Professor J. G. C. Anderson

THE area which includes the two portions of the Forest Park is as definitely Highland from a geological point of view as it is in respect of geography, scenery and vegetation. The various types of rocks that occur are representative of those which build up most of the country between the Firth of Clyde and the Great Glens containing Loch Linnhe and Loch Ness. The interpretation of the structure of the most ancient of these rocks provided the key to an understanding of the formation of the south-west Highlands as a whole. Further, in the Forest Park area, as throughout the Highlands, there is abundant evidence of a comparatively recent glaciation which has had characteristic effects upon the topography and superficial deposits.

Most of the region is underlain by metamorphic rocks. These were originally sediments, such as impure sandstones, shales,

27

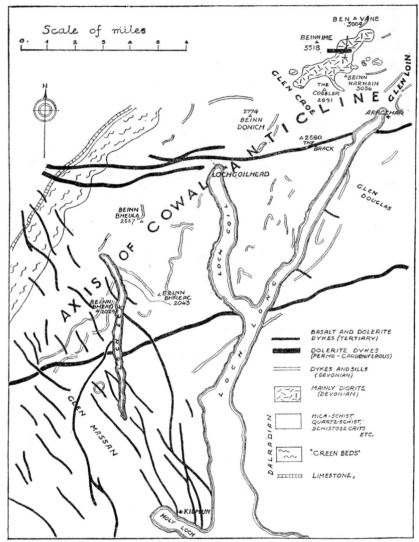

Fig. 1—Geological Sketch Map.

limestones, etc., but at one or more times in their history they were subjected to intense heat and pressure which greatly altered both their mineral composition and their structure. In general these metamorphic rocks may be recognised by the presence of marked cleavage or foliation, which causes them to split very readily in one direction and even in the unbroken state to appear divided into thin parallel bands.

In addition to the metamorphic rocks the region provides us with examples of various types of primary or igneous rocks. These have been formed by the consolidation of molten material which has risen from the depths and has been forced into cavities and fissures in the earth's crust. The igneous rocks, although varying widely among themselves, may be distinguished from the metamorphic rocks by their more homogeneous nature, by their close welded appearance, and by the absence of cleavage or foliation.

Excluding the glacial deposits, which are still loose and uncompacted, the region shows no rocks other than metamorphic and igneous types. Part of the history of the area in comparatively recent geological times can, however, be made out from a study of the valley system, and the effect of the glaciation upon these.

THE METAMORPHIC ROCKS

The metamorphic rocks belong to the well-known Dalriadian system. This occupies a large proportion of the country between the Highland Boundary Fault, a great break in the earth's crust crossing Scotland from Stonehaven to Rothesay, and another major fracture which determines the course of the Great Glen and Loch Linnhe. In the Forest Park the Dalriadian system is represented mainly by various kinds of schistose grit and mica-schist. Thoroughly typical examples of mica-schist may be seen on The Cobbler and are noteworthy for their extremely well-marked foliation, for the minor puckers and folds into which the latter is often contorted, and for their beautiful silvery sheen due to the abundance of flakes of glittering muscovite or white mica. The schistose grits contain a much higher proportion of quartz, have a dull white appearance and are often gritty. They occur throughout the area, and are particularly strongly developed on either side of the mouth of Loch Goil and at the north-east end of Loch Eck. Good sections in interbedded schistose grit and mica schist may be seen along the Rest-and-be-Thankful road to Glen Croe.

North-west of Loch Eck the schistose grits and mica schists are succeeded by a rather puzzling group referred to as the "Green Beds", the colour of which is due to the presence of such minerals as chlorite and epidote which are richer in iron and magnesium than white mica. Then at the boundary of the Park, and just south of where the River Cur bends sharply north-west, is exposed a band of altered and re-crystallised limestone. This band, which is spoken of as the Loch Tay limestone, although comparatively thin, has been traced to the north-east far into the central Highlands.

29

All these rocks were involved at the close of Silurian times in major horizontal movements of the earth's crust accompanying what is known as the Caledonian period of mountain-building. This brought into existence a great chain, with a general north-east trend, in Scotland and Scandinavia. At first sight this seems only to have produced a great arch or anticline. Thus along the zone marked in Fig. 1 "Axis of Cowal Anticline" (for example, near the middle of Loch Eck and on The Cobbler), the rock surfaces will be seen to appear like a pack of cards lying flat; to the north-west (for example, in the valley of the River Cur) like a pack of cards sloping north-west; and to the south-east (for example, near the Holy Loch) like a pack of cards sloping south-east. It was first realised by the geologist Clough, however, that this interpretation was too simple and did not fit the facts. The opposite sides of the arch did not match. Clough was able to show that the rocks of the district had first of all been forced into a flat-lying fold, almost like a piece of paper doubled over, and that it was this fold that had later been bent into an arch. A little consideration, or experiment with pieces of paper, will show that in such a flat-lying or "recumbent" fold, as it is called, the beds in the lower "limb" must be in inverted order. This is believed to be the case with all the strata in the north-east part of the area. The Loch Tay limestone and Green Beds, originally below the misca-schist and grits, have now come to rest on top of them. No absolute proof of this has so far been forthcoming in Cowal, but lest it be thought that such wholesale over-turnings of Highland strata are impossible, it may be mentioned that they have been proved beyond doubt in the Loch Leven district farther north.

The age of these Dalriadian rocks, which are quite unfossiliferous, is unknown, but the Caledonian mountain-building movements are believed to have taken place some 350 million years ago.

THE LOWER OLD RED SANDSTONE ROCKS

In the extreme north-east of Fig. 1 will be noticed one large and several smaller outcrops of "diorite". These are masses of igneous rock which by comparison with similar intrusions of known age farther to the north are believed to have been injected in Old Red Sandstone or Devonian times. The largest mass of diorite may be well seen immediately north of Beinn Narnain, from where it descends to form a long exposure in the Allt Coiregrogain, and in the stream to the north-west of The Cobbler. The diorite really includes a variety of rocks, all of which are fairly basic, that is rich in iron and magnesium, and of a dark colour. In the centre of the largest mass, between Beinn Narnain and the head of the Allt

Coiregrogain, is an intrusion of granite (not large enough to be shown in Fig. 1), which is light grey or pink in colour. The diorite seems to have given rise to much softer topography than the schist, which often rises as crags above it. In addition to the diorite, in Old Red Sandstone times, liquid rock was injected into narrow fissures which, if approximately horizontal, gave rise to *sills* and, if vertical, to *dykes*. These may be seen almost throughout the Park and consist for the most part of fine pinkish or greyish compact rocks known as porphyries and lamprophyres. Several thin lamprophyre sills may be seen along the new Rest-and-be-Thankful road, not far from the summit.

IGNEOUS ROCKS LATER THAN THE OLD RED SANDSTONE

In Fig. 1 will be noticed a few broad persistent dykes with an east-west trend. These consist of the blackish, medium-grained basic rock dolerite and are outlying examples of a number of such dykes which were injected for the most part in the Midland Valley of Scotland in late Carboniferous or early Permian times. Then in the south-west of the area will be seen a large "swarm" of dykes all of which have a general north-west trend. These are the youngest solid rocks of the region. They consist of dolerite or of the similar but finer grained rock basalt and may be traced to a focus in the great Tertiary igneous centre of Mull.

TOPOGRAPHY

The striking relief of the district is not the direct result of the upheavals that have been described. The scenery, as throughout Scotland, is the result of sculpture. The mountains are what has been left of an elevated, south-easterly sloping plateau deeply intersected by numerous valleys. The valleys to begin with followed the slope of the tableland and are believed to have carried the headstreams, first of a primitive River Tweed following what is now the Clyde valley above Glasgow and continuing through the Biggar Gap, and later of an enlarged River Forth. Relics of these old "consequent" valleys, as they are termed, may be seen in the continuation of Glen Croe by the Tarbet Gap, Coilessan Glen by Glen Douglas, etc. As time went on they were intercepted by the present valley system and directed into the River Clyde. Several of the present valleys are occupied by deep narrow lochs of the fiord type, *e.g.* Loch Long. According to one view the fiords are the result of faulting or fissuring during a late uplift. They are, however, more likely to have been river valleys scooped out into deep basins by glaciers and transformed into sea lochs by a submergence of the land.

31

GLACIATION

The chief effect of the glaciation was to modify the existing valleys, not to produce new ones. This modification characteristically took the form of "over deepening", so that on the retreat of the ice the tributary valleys which had formerly been "in grade" with the main valleys now had to drop steeply into them. A glaciated valley is in fact typically U-shaped compared with the V-shaped valley due purely to river erosion, and much more open, as spurs which originally projected into it were ground back by the ice. A magnificent example of such a glaciated valley may be seen by looking down the Allt Coiregrogain from the col between The Cobbler and Beinn Ime. Glaciers sometimes form corries, or rounded hollows up on a mountain. Three such corries are to be seen on the Ben More Range.

Another effect of the glaciation is seen in the deposits of clay, sand and gravel, mixed with boulders, which cover a large part of the area. Often these occur in well-marked mounds, termed moraines, for example in the valley of the Allt Coire Odhair (north-east of Lochgoilhead) and in Glenbranter.

POST-GLACIAL GEOLOGICAL CHANGES

The last of the glaciers disappeared perhaps only 12,000 years ago. The operation of geological changes since that period is seen in the great tumbled masses of landslipped material which occur on many of the hill-sides (for instance on the Glen Croe face of The Cobbler, also on the west side of the middle of Loch Eck) and in the deltas which many of the rivers have built out into the lochs, as at the mouth of Glen Croe, where the Ardgartan camp site now stands.

Sheets of the Geological Survey 1-inch to the mile map of Scotland showing parts of the area are Nos. 29, 37 and 38.

Geological Survey Memoirs dealing with parts of the area are:

CLOUGH, C.T.   1897: *The Geology of Cowal.*
HILL, J. B.   1905: *The Geology of Mid-Argyll.* (Explanation of Sheet 37).
READ, H. H.   1935: *British Regional Geology: The Grampian Highlands.*

Butterwort, Cotton grass, Globe flower and Bog bean.

Today, last season's butterwort
lay like stranded starfish
on the sea-green moss;
the hart's-tongue fern
stood embalmed within the stillness
of the derelict limekiln;
first shoots of primrose foliage
were fresh beneath the leafless alders
and pied wagtails made nervous flights
between shore and shrub.

—Charles Senior.

PLANT LIFE IN THE PARK

By Professor John Walton and W. B. Ribbons

On the surface of the land moulded by mountain-building movements and left bare with the retreat of the glaciers some 10,000 years
ago, the present vegetation developed, and is still undergoing slow
changes. When the land reappeared from beneath its covering of ice
the rocky slopes and deposits of detrital material were colonised by
plants, most of which must have migrated from the south, although a
few arctic-alpine species may have existed during the last glaciation
on some of the peaks which stood above the ice-sheet.

On the soils formed by these pioneers, including lichens, mosses, herbs, dwarf shrubs, willows and birch, forests and, later, moorlands developed. There is clear evidence from microscopic remains of plants preserved in lake muds and peats and also from tree stumps in peats that the area which includes the Forest Park was more densely wooded than at present. Over the last 5,500 years and especially in the last 500 years man and grazing animals have been largely responsible for the destruction of the original forests, only traces of which are left.

The Park area is deeply cut into by sea lochs, and with the exception of parts of the Ben More range of mountains to the west of Loch Eck there are no parts of it which are more than four miles from sea water. It is therefore a region where, with the exception of the higher ground, the mean annual temperature is relatively high. The lower levels surrounding the lochs are rarely subject to severe frosts. In the magnificent gardens of Benmore House the visitor may see many exotic flowering shrubs and such plants as eucalyptus and palms flourishing out-of-doors. The rainfall is high. At Benmore House for instance the average annual rainfall is about 100 inches, while at the Arrochar end of the Park it is not less than 130 inches. Such climatic conditions favour the growth of cone-bearing trees.

MARINE VEGETATION

The coasts of Loch Long and Loch Goil are for the most part rocky, but owing to their narrowness the wave action on the shores is not nearly so severe as that of the more open Firth of Clyde. As a result we find on the rocks exposed at low tide a dense covering of sea-weeds, red, brown and green, which offer an interesting study to the botanist. There is practically no sand dune or salt marsh vegetation in the Park.

VEGETATION OF THE VALLEYS AND LOWER SLOPES

Perhaps the most striking feature of the vegetation to the visitor from other parts of Great Britain is the exceptionally rich flora of lichens, bryophytes (mosses and liverworts) and ferns, linked with the abundant rainfall. Practically all rock surfaces removed from the splash of salt water from shore level to the highest summits, are encrusted with lichens or festooned with bryophytes, and the varied colouring these plants bring to the scene is quite remarkable.

The river valleys contain some cultivated and pasture land, and on the river banks and in marshy areas woods of alder, willow, birch and ash are found, along with a rich meadow and river bank flora of herbs in which meadowsweet (*Filipendula ulmaria*) and whorled caraway (*Carum verticillatum*) are characteristic. Loch Eck is an

34

exceptionally fine example of a Highland freshwater loch and contains a representative flora of aquatic species including water lobelia (*Lobelia dortmanna*), water-milfoil (*Myriophyllum* spp), pond weeds (*Potamogeton* spp), quillwort (*Isoetes lacustris*), horsetails (*Equisetum* spp), stoneworts (*Charophyta* spp) and a fairly rich shallow water and marginal flora.

The land rises in most places fairly steeply from the shore and at lower levels bears woodland. The natural woods of the district consist of alder, willow and birch in the wetter or marshy parts, and oak, ash, birch, hazel, elm, rowan and holly on the better drained ground. Scots pine occurs in places but may have been re-introduced; it grows better in the drier climate of the east of Scotland. The herbaceous flora of the woods appears at its best in spring and early summer before the trees have developed their canopy of foliage. Large areas may be found covered with wild hyacinths, primroses, anemones and violets; the small shrubby blaeberry (*Vaccinium myrtillus*) is also abundant.

On drier slopes there are large bracken-covered areas, and heathland in which ling heather (*Calluna vulgaris*) and bell heather (*Erica cinerea*) are the dominant elements in the vegetation. In the wetter parts of the heather-covered areas the cross-leaved heath (*Erica tetralix*) is to be found.

On level areas moorland vegetation consisting of grasses and sedges forms a characteristic covering; sometimes the purple moorgrass (*Molinia caerulea*) dominates, with an admixture of cross-leaved heath, the yellow flowered bog asphodel (*Narthecium ossifragum*) and the heath spotted-orchid (*Dactylorhiza maculata*). In places there may be extensive thickets of the bog myrtle (*Myrica gale*), a shrub whose purple twigs give a bright colour to the landscape in winter, and whose aromatic green shoots are the badge of the Clan Campbell.

On the wet banks of the streams the insectivorous round-leaved sundew (*Drosera rotundifolia*) and common butterwort (*Pinguicula vulgaris*) and the showy yellow saxifrage (*Saxifraga aizoides*) are frequent. In shaded ravines and on wet rocks filmy-ferns (*Hymenophyllum* spp) with their small translucent fronds are often found among the mosses, from which they are not readily distinguished at first sight.

VEGETATION OF THE HIGHER SLOPES AND MOORLAND

Oak woodland does not extend above about 800 feet but the woods of birch with occasional rowan and holly may extend to greater altitudes. Bracken (*Pteridium aquilinum*) and heather are not usually found above 2,000 feet and are gradually replaced by an increasing amount of dwarfed blaeberry and cowberry (*Vaccinium vitis-idaea*). The upper slopes are grassy and here the clubmosses (*Lycopodium selago* and *L. clavatum*) occur.

On the more level ground and on the tops of the rounded mountains at about 2,000 feet there may be peat moors on which grasses, small sedges and the rushes such as the heath rush (*Juncus squarrosus*) are abundant. On the very wet parts at all levels, cottongrasses (*Eriophorum* spp) with their white cottony fruits are conspicuous and the bogs are largely covered with bogmoss (*Sphagnum* spp).

Plants of the crowberry (*Empetrum nigrum*) and commonly of the mountain crowberry (*E. hermaphroditum*) and the cloudberry (*Rubus chamaemorus*) occasionally occur in patches. Above 2,000 feet on the well-drained slopes the grassland contains alpine meadow-rue (*Thalictrum alpinum*), the alpine lady's-mantle (*Alchemilla alpina*), mountain everlasting (*Antennaria dioica*), alpine clubmoss (*Lycopodium alpinum*), and the moss campion (*Silene acaulis*) whose green cushion-like masses of small shoots are covered with bright pink blossom in early summer. Among the rarer species are the alpine lady-fern (*Athyrium distentifolium*), the holly fern (*Polystichum lonchitis*), the bog bilberry (*Vaccinium uliginosum*) and alpine saw-wort (*Saussurea alpina*).

In the stream gorges and in the corries, so characteristic of glaciated mountains, a rich flora is to be found, for in such situations occur plants which elsewhere on the mountains may be found both at higher and lower altitudes. Perhaps the most conspicuous are the globeflower (*Trollius europaeus*) with its large golden yellow flowers, the goldenrod (*Solidago virgaurea*), several species of saxifrage, including the purple saxifrage (*Saxifraga oppositifolia*) and the roseroot (*Sedum rosea*).

The tutsan (*Hypericum androsaemum*), the slender St. John's-wort (*H. pulchrum*), and the oak and beech ferns (*Gymnocarpium dryopteris* and *Thelypteris phegopteris*) are frequent here and elsewhere in the Park.

On the summits over 1,700 feet one may usually find the dwarf willow (*Salix herbacea*) and the three-leaved rush (*Juncus trifidus*) growing among the mosses and in the crevices of the rocks. A similar flora to that occurring in the stream gorges is to be found on the rock ledges in the precipitous corries, particularly those with a northern aspect. Magnificent clumps of globeflower, purple saxifrage and moss campion may sometimes be seen on the more inaccessible ledges.

The Park contains a fine variety of the types of vegetation characteristic of the western Scottish Highlands, from the marine vegetation of the coast up to the arctic-alpine vegetation of the summits. Although there may not be many of the rarer Scottish plants, there is indeed sufficient variety to please the eyes of all who take pleasure in natural beauty and to satisfy the naturalist who will find immense scope for study and investigation.

It is to be hoped that those who visit the Park will take a keen interest in its plant life and will help to preserve its botanical treasures from damage and extinction. If spotted-orchids, for example, are picked because they are plentiful they will soon cease to be so; if the rarer species are picked they will quickly disappear altogether. Leave the plants for others to enjoy. For identification, take the smallest possible bit; but often a photograph may serve the purpose. The uprooting of any wild plant, throughout the Forest Park, is naturally forbidden under the Forestry Commission's bye-laws.

BIBLIOGRAPHY

LEE, JOHN R. 1908: *The flora of the Arrochar mountains*. Annals Andersonian Naturalists' Society. Vol. III.

LEE, J. R. 1933: *The flora of the Clyde area*. Glasgow.

NISBET, T. 1911: *The plant geography of Ardgoil*. Scottish Geographical Magazine. Vol. XXVII.

NISBET, I. 1914: *Phanerogams and ferns of South Ardgoil*. Annals Andersonian Naturalists' Society. Vol. IV.

Thou man who travellest blithely
Nor hurt nor harm shall befall thee
Nor in sunshine nor in darkness
If but the club-moss be on thy pathway.
　　　　　　—Carbhag an t'Sleibhe, *The Club Moss.*

Twelve-pointer Stag

To call a bird a bird, a tree a tree
Is insufficient for his earnest mind—
These words are symbols only, mute and blind.
Shape, colour, texture, sound identify
A bird, a tree, a singing in the air
Precisely. From a feather he restores
Heartbeat and cry and dappled spread of wing;
From slender lizard's imprint on the grass
His careful mind can reconstruct and bring
The shadows back, and see the creature there.
                    —Margaret Reynolds: *The Naturalist.*

ANIMALS AND BIRDS
OF THE FOREST PARK

By D. Henderson and M. Yorke

THE forests and mountainous land of the Argyll Forest Park provide
a wide variety of habitats for an interesting variety of animal and
bird species. The following account can only give the visitor a brief
insight into the wildlife that can be enjoyed from both sight and
sound. A true and lively picture can of course best be obtained if
the visitor, complete with fieldglasses, walks quietly along the forest

roads or over the hillsides in the early hours of daylight or in the hour before dusk. While doing so please cause as little disturbance as possible—particularly during the breeding season—for both your own and other visitors' benefit.

Consider the wealth and variety of wildlife that forestry has helped to establish on ground that originally was predominately open windswept sheep grazings. There are probably very few localities in the British Isles where there is an opportunity to see such a wide variety within a comparatively compact area of countryside; providing habitats which range from the sea and freshwater lochs and burns; through low ground agricultural land and marshes; into the forest of a variety of tree species and ages and out on to the open broadleaf scrub woodland; before reaching the open hill land of grass and heather and up to the mountain tops over 2,000 feet high. In the space available it is not possible to mention all of the many species of animals and birds within the Forest Park but we hope this account will be sufficient to encourage visitors to look more closely and enjoy the sight or sound perhaps, of a species they have not seen before.

ANIMALS

The largest animal in the Park is the red deer which is established throughout the area and can be found on the high mountain slopes or in the shelter of the plantations. This shelter, combined with the rich grass and other herbage which grows within the plantation fences following the exclusion of grazing sheep or cattle results in the red deer growing to a larger size compared with the deer of the more exposed and treeless areas of the Highlands further north. Probably the most exciting time to see these fine animals is during late September and October when the stags collect their harem of hinds together during the rutting season and the noise of their "roaring" challenge can be heard echoing down the glens.

The smaller and less conspicuous roe deer is comparatively common throughout the Park and is more often found within the plantations or broadleaved scrub areas and less frequently out on the open hillsides. The deep bark of an alarmed roe deer may often be heard whilst walking quietly through the forests. Unlike the red deer, they spend much of the year in family groups of the doe and her twin kids. The only time when this graceful animal is unpopular is when it takes a liking to a gardener's prize collection of roses or strawberry plants, particularly in the spring.

Both species cause browsing damage to trees in young plantations, while the males will rub the bark off saplings while marking out their territory or annually removing the old velvet that covers their newly grown antlers. As adult deer have virtually no natural predators their numbers would increase rapidly in the shelter provided by the forest. To prevent damage to the young trees becoming severe their numbers are kept under control by the Forestry Commission's highly trained and experienced rangers. This also ensures the maintenance within the forest of a healthy population of these fine animals.

Blackcock and Wild cat

The larger predatory animals within the Park are the wild cat, badger, fox and otter. All except the otter can be found both within the forest plantations and out on the open hillsides. The otter is probably the rarest of these four species and is restricted to the few rivers and burns that run into the sea lochs within the park boundary. All of these predators are most likely to be seen during dusk as they set off on their nightly hunting expedition, or as they return at dawn—the wild cat to his "lair" in a rocky cairn with his meal of rabbit, hare, grouse or field vole; the badger to his "sett" in a dry woodland glade after a meal of frogs, wasp nest or beetles; the fox to his "earth" in a rocky cairn or sandy hole with a meal of rabbit, shrew, pheasant or stillborn deer calf; the otter to his "holt" in a large old tree root on the river bank after his meal of fish or frog.

The best time of year to see these animals is during the early summer when the adults are busily feeding their young throughout

Plate 17. Southward prospect across Loch Goil from Lochgoilhead, which is seen on the left.

Plate 18. The high road through Glen Croe climbs the Rest-and-be-thankful Pass on its way towards Inveraray.

Plate 19.   Heron watching a still pool on the River Echaig, close to Benmore House.

Plate 20.   Winter snows outline the rugged summit of Clach Bheinn, seen across Loch Ecl from Whistlefield.

Plate 21. Puck's Glen. This fascinating cleft in the rocks, close to Benmore House, is the haunt of rare ferns, mosses and liverworts. A footpath follows its gurgling stream.

Plate 22.   Panorama of the Argyll Forest Park, viewed from Gourock across the broad Firth of Clyde, which flows seawards from right to left of the picture. In the distance are the Holy Loch (*left*), Benmore Forest (*centre*), and the entrance to Loch Long (*right*). The Cross of Lorraine (*left foreground*) commemorates Free French Seamen who fought in

Plate 23. Looking down on the delta of the River Croe, near the head of Loch Long, showing the Ardgartan Camping Ground spread out on its shingle bank.

Plate 24. A teacher demonstrates soil pit profiles to a group of students on a field study course.

Plate 25. Where the Massan joins the Echaig; a water meeting in Benmore Forest, near Dunoon.

Plate 26. The rare moss campion, *Silene acaulis*, an alpine plant found on the high peaks near Arrochar.

Plate 27. Intricate turf on a Park hillside: Ling heather, *Calluna vulgaris* (*left*) and cross-leaved heath, *Erica tetralix* (*right*).

Plate 28. Yellow globe flower, *Trollius europaeus*, flourishes along streamsides.

much of the mornings and evenings and when the young emerge from below ground to romp and play and are still too young to appreciate the dangers of man's presence.

All these predators have benefited from the shelter and seclusion created by the establishment of forest plantations within the Park, which has itself increased the numbers and variety of other wild animals and birds on which these species prey. Although the fox and wild cat are not enemies of the forester, indeed their ability to control populations of rabbits, hares and voles is beneficial, they can cause trouble for the sheep farmer during the lambing season when sickly lambs may be attacked.

The smaller predatory animals are the stoat and weasel which feed on nestling birds and rabbits and shrews. They are not frequently seen and appear restricted to the lower agricultural ground and surrounding woodland. Perhaps by the time this Guide is next written we will be able to record the presence of a pine marten within the Park. Closely related to the stoat and weasel, it is a comparatively rare animal found in the remoter parts of the old pine forests further north. A few unconfirmed reports have been received of this shy and elusive animal being seen in Argyll.

The rabbit is usually to be found on the lower ground and particularly on the fringes of agricultural ground with the forest. Its numbers fluctuate rapidly as a result of the periodic recurrence of the myxomatosis disease and it forms a significant part of the diet of many of the predatory animals and birds within the Park.

Both the brown hare found in a few places on the low agricultural ground and occasionally within the forest, and the blue hare found on the open hills and mountains, also provide part of the menu for the fox, wild cat or golden eagle. The blue hare is comparatively uncommon in this part of Scotland and like the stoat it changes from its blue/grey colour in summer to almost pure white in winter in an effort to camouflage itself in the harsh environment amongst the high and exposed mountainsides.

The grey squirrel, which as an introduction to Britain in the 1880s has done so much damage to forestry and horticulture in the southern parts of the country, was introduced in 1892 to the area around Finnart on the east shore of Loch Long. Probably as a result of the wet climate and the absence of extensive areas of nut-bearing broadleaf woodlands, it has failed to spread widely beyond the eastern fringe of the Park. Meanwhile its more attractive relation the red squirrel, can still be found in a few places through the Park where areas of oak, beech and hazel scrub woodland occur.

The initial stage in the establishment of a forest plantation result in the area being fenced off from grazing sheep and cattle. As a

41

result the grass and heather grows vigorously between the plough furrows at 6 or 7 feet apart on which the young trees are planted, and this regrowth of herbage provides shelter and food for a variety of small rodents such as the field vole, field mouse and shrew. A sharp increase or "explosion" of their population occurs and even in a hard winter with snow on the ground the thick matted grass—which is absent if sheep are grazing the area—provides shelter and protection. As a consequence of their population increase, the number of predatory birds and animals which prey upon these small creatures, also increases. In particular, the various species of owls, the kestrel, the sparrow hawk, the buzzard and the hen harrier all increase in numbers—at least until such time as the young trees grow up and close canopy and shade out the grass and other ground vegetation amongst which their prey is to be found. By that time, however, another area of forest will have been established elsewhere and the same cycle of events continues.

This one very simple example of the effect of forestry on the population dynamics of a wild life population, is repeated in the varied stages of the 50–60 year life of a coniferous forest—each stage of which provides the food and shelter for a changing number and variety of birds and animals.

BIRDS

The tawny and barn owl are both found in the Park usually on the lower ground and on the fringes between agriculture and the forest. An old derelict farm building as well as an old hole-ridden tree provide their nesting and roosting places. The long-eared owl with its two long feather tufts on either side of its head is the rarest of the four owl species to be seen. It tends to frequent the forest more than the open ground and hunts at night and is more likely to be found in the older larch plantations or broadleaf woodland where it nests on the ground at the base of a tree in the bracken. There have been no reports of the little owl in the Park, but the short-eared owl is comparatively common, particularly amongst the newly planted plantations, for the reasons already mentioned. It hunts by day and at dusk, and its slow flapping wing beats as it quarters close to the ground are characteristic.

The kestrel performing its hovering flight with tail fanned out and occasional rapid wing beats, can often be seen hunting for prey either above farmland or above young plantations and out on the open hill. Its shrill courtship or "playing" call of "kee-kee-kee", readily identifies it from the larger sparrow hawk which hunts by rapid darting low level flight amongst the treetops and along the roads and ride sides in its efforts to surprise small song birds.

The buzzard and hen harrier appear both to have increased in numbers over the years. The former nests in mature conifer or broadleaf woodland, and is often to be seen soaring in slow wide circles at a great height in the warm thermal currents of a summer's day or hunting for rabbits or field mice on the low ground farmland. The hen harrier nests on the ground amongst the heather outside the plantations or within a young plantation that has not yet closed canopy. It keeps to the high ground and hunts for prey of vole or nestling bird with a slow wing beat, flying at less than fifty feet above the ground.

Probably the two most noteworthy birds of prey within the Park are the golden eagle and peregrine. Both have their eyries or nesting places in high and often inaccessible rocky crags with a commanding view of the surrounding countryside. The eagle with a seven-feet wing span can occasionally be seen in summer as it soars above the mountain tops and can be distinguished from the buzzard by its larger size and black bar on the underside and end of its tail.

Red grouse and Golden eagle

The peregrine, of similar size to the kestrel, appears also to be increasing in numbers as a result amongst other things of the vigilance of the Forestry Commission Rangers in their attempts to shield it and other rare species from the depredation of the egg collector. It is difficult to identify from the kestrel or sparrow hawk at a distance, but the tremendous speed of stoop or dive at its prey of grouse or pigeon is a spectacular sight on the open mountainside.

Other bird species that can be found on the high ground above 600 feet and outside the forest areas, include two game birds—red grouse feeding on the heather and bilberry ground, and its close relation the ptarmigan which is found in small numbers above about 2,000 feet and survives on the heather and lichen growth. It is the one bird species in the Park that changes colour from mottled brown in summer to almost pure white in winter in an effort to camouflage itself against the preying eagle or fox

In spring and summer the curlew, skylark, meadow pipit, snipe, twite, stonechat and wheatear can all be found nesting on the ground amongst the rough hill grassland outside the plantations. As winter approaches they move to lower ground or further south in the country, with the two waders the snipe and curlew moving to the lower marshes and shores of the sea lochs. The "drumming" courtship display of the snipe and the shrill clear bubbling call of the curlew are familiar sounds in summer, while an occasional view of a ring ousel may occur above 1,000 feet as it skulks timidly amongst the rocks, looking similar to a blackbird but with a white crest on its chest.

Finally, three other birds that frequent the open hill and mountain grazings of the Park, are the raven and hooded and carrion crow, all of which live mainly off the carrion provided by dead or dying animals, together with eggs and nestling birds. The largest of the three is the jet black raven whose coarse croaking call can be heard high in the sky as it engages in a courtship display of a rolling, twisting dive with wings half closed and often flying upside down. It is the earliest bird to breed and starts to lay its eggs in February in a nest of sticks, heather and wool, high up on an inaccessible rocky crag.

The hooded and carrion crows are closely related and renowned scavengers of carrion and destroyers of many birds' nests. As a result, their numbers are restricted by the Rangers as far as is practicable, but with a ready supply of food from carrion on the hill during summer and shell fish on the lochsides in winter, they will continue to thrive.

Within the forest of both coniferous and broadleaf trees, and on its fringes with the adjoining agricultural ground, there is a wide variety of predominately song birds which thrive as a result of both the shelter from predators and the climate, and the increased insect food supply provided by the tree growth.

Of the game birds that can be found, are the occasional pheasants on the low ground adjoining the agricultural fields. These are survivors of the days when, over 50 years ago, a number of the original landowners employed gamekeepers to maintain a sporting estate, before selling the ground for forestry after the decline of sheep farming. The black grouse, the male bird of which is the blackcock and the female the greyhen, is comparatively common on the higher fringes of the forest where it borders with the heather-clad hillside. The male birds are a magnificent sight as they congregate at dawn in May and June for their courtship display or "lek", which takes place on the same grassy knoll each year.

Within the forest itself, particularly in the moister parts of scrub woodland or a larch plantation, can be found the woodcock whose courtship flight, known as "roding", together with a froglike croak, can often be seen or heard in a forest ride during dusk in the summer months. One other game bird to be found only infrequently is the magnificent capercaillie which is more typically found in the mature pine forests in the drier eastern parts of Scotland. However, this large bird, which is often known as a forest turkey, has recently shown signs of trying to establish itself in the forests of the Park, and the male bird has displayed typical examples of his aggression as he attacks the forester or his vehicle as he makes his way to work.

The list of smaller birds to be found within the forests of the Park is large, and cannot be described in this short account. They are chiefly but not entirely insect eating species with some being summer breeding migrant visitors but the majority being annual residents. The list includes the green and great-spotted woodpeckers, the treecreeper, goldfinch, chiffchaff, wood warbler, garden warbler, willow warbler, wren, great tit, blue tit, long-tailed tit, coal tit, spotted flycatcher, goldcrest, cuckoo, pied and yellow wagtails as well as all the common resident and migratory species one finds in a rural garden in northern Britain, such as the chaffinch, greenfinch, bullfinch, blackbird, thrush, robin, etc. Also one must not overlook the colourful jay and magpie, both of which prey upon eggs and fledgelings in addition to carrion in the case of the magpie, and beech and hazel nuts for example in the case of the jay. Wood pigeons also frequents the forests and surrounding farm land, but in small numbers compared with the large flocks seen on agricultural ground further south. The collared dove, one of the more recent breeding arrivals to the British Isles from Europe, can be found in small numbers in gardens on the southern fringe of the Park and on at least one cereal-producing farm.

An extensive habitat for animals and birds within the boundaries of the Park is provided by the fresh water and sea water lochs, providing excellent opportunities to see a variety of ducks, waders and seabirds. The largest examples being the mute swans which breed on the edges of the lochs, the whooper swan which visits the area during the winter from northern Europe and the heron which is resident throughout the year and can often be seen on the lochside poised to spear a fish or frog.

Of the wildfowl, mallard, teal, wigeon, eider, tufted duck, goosander, and red-breasted merganser are all common breeding or winter visiting species, while the less common pochard, goldeneye and shelduck also occur.

Oystercatchers in flight, Redshanks and Curlew

In addition to the waders and other water birds mentioned earlier, the moorhen, lapwing, common sandpiper, dipper, redshank and oystercatcher all breed within the Park. All the common species of gull occur on the lochs and seasonal visitors include the occasional red and black-throated divers, the cormorant, common tern, arctic tern and gannet whose plummeting dive into the loch is an exciting sight as it fishes for mackerel to take back to its young on the rocky island of Ailsa Craig in the Firth of Clyde.

Other birds to look out for are the skeins of greylag and pinkfoot geese, en route to and from their breeding ground in Iceland and

Greenland, which rarely land within the Park itself while heading east to the Perthshire farmland and lochs or south to the Solway mudflats. Winter visitors from further north include the flocks of fieldfares and redwings that come to feed on the rowan and holly berries. Flocks of linnets and snowbuntings may also be seen. The crossbill, hitherto only a northern visitor, has recently been recorded as a breeding resident in the Park. It has a uniquely formed beak designed to tear open tree cones so that it can reach the seeds on which it feeds.

This account has provided an insight into the wealth of wildlife that may be seen during the year amidst the magnificent scenery of the Forest Park. Please give it the protection which it deserves, and also for the future enjoyment of all.

Remember you will be better able to observe and appreciate the wild life of this Forest Park if you increase your knowledge and understanding of them. This can be achieved by reading books or publications—your local librarian will advise; or by joining natural history societies or wild life trusts. If you wish to develop a special interest then seek out and join the appropriate society—these are too many and varied to be fully chronicled here but some well known examples are The British Trust for Ornithology, The British Deer Society, and The British Mammals Society.

When Deirdre brought her sorrow
she won the sea birds native of this isle
with her brave lament
for still they cry her elegy
along these sacred shores.

—Charles Senior.

Atlantic grey seal

And bending southwards
with stems of sea-thrift,
safely rooted on the tide-pocked rocks,
you gazed in steep wonder
on the magic symmetry
of jelly-fish lapping
the plankton fulness
of the high tide.

—Charles Senior.

MARINE AND FRESHWATER LIFE
By H. D. Slack

For the study of aquatic life the Argyll Park has the distinction and good fortune, among Forest Parks, to be bounded for nearly half of its extent by the sea. Standing bodies of freshwater are less extensive and few in number: about three miles of the western side of Loch Lomond: the six mile stretch of Loch Eck: the very much smaller Loch Restil and two lochans high in the hills. The small rivers, Loin, Goil and Eachaig, with numerous hill streams comprise the running water.

THE SEA SHORE

The sea shore has prior claim to our attention by virtue of its extent. Where life on earth began, the sea, has evolved a diversity of animals (but a lesser diversity of plants) that is quite unapproached by that of freshwaters. The multitude of animals, from the weakly swimming and generally small inhabitants that drift at the mercy of currents in the open sea (which, together with microscopic plants, constitute the plankton), through the rich fauna of invertebrates and fishes associated with the sea bed, to pelagic fishes and marine mammals, makes it impossible to encompass more than a small proportion of them here. Moreover, elaborate equipment is required for the study of the open water. This account will deal principally with what you are likely to find along the shore between high and low tide levels; bringing in the plankton where it is involved, since many of the shore animals start their lives as temporary members of it.

It is frankly an account based on a personal and rather cursory survey such as the ordinary visitor might be expected to make, and a deeper insight is given by the excellent and delightfully illustrated books on marine life quoted at the end of this chapter.

In contrast to the constant conditions for life, enjoyed by the plankton and pelagic fishes, that the open sea offers, the continual and drastic changes of the sea shore result in an environment having an inconsistency such as is to be found nowhere else.

The advance and retreat of the tide, varying in height throughout the month from a maximum at springs to a minimum at neaps, means that all life there must be adapted to living in and out of water for varying periods from twice a day to once a month.

The problems which must be solved and have been solved by the inhabitants of this inconstant environment are how to avoid dessication, how to withstand quick changes of temperature and the alternation of low oxygen content in water too high in air, and how to guard against the dangers of being swept away or killed by dashing waves.

The sea bed on which they live presents a variety of habitats: rock faces with clefts and crannies and rock pools, when the tide is low, or broken down rock ranging from boulders and smaller stones down to sand.

All of these may be found on the sea loch shores of the Park but rock faces with pools are very limited in extent. They occur at Strone on the Kilmun shore. Extensive areas of clear sand are also infrequent but are to be found at the heads of the Holy Loch and Loch Goil.

For the most part the intertidal shores are made up of stones set in gravels and sand. Stones that range in size up to large boulders. The gently shelving shore at the head of Loch Long is largely cobble stones set in sand but strewn with boulders as one proceeds south to

49

Ardgartan and Coilessan. Along the Holy Loch and Loch Long from Kilmun round to Gairletter the shore is similar, with the exception of the Strone rock faces; while Loch Goil has a fairly steeply inclined boulder slope apart from the sand area.

It is the seaweeds on boulders and stones, draped down in masses when the tide is out, together with crevices under stones, that provide the humid conditions (and concealment from predatory gulls) needed by the animals. When the tide is in they form a miniature forest and are then a haven from the force of the waves. The familiar seaweeds are classified as green algae (*Chlorophyceae*), brown algae (*Phaeophyceae*) and red algae (*Rhodophyceae*) but, in appearance, their colour may sometimes belie the name.

Distribution of the various weeds down the shore is in accordance with their adaptation to the degree of exposure between tides. Small pools, rendered brackish by drainage at the landward margin, are favoured by the bright green, delicate, fronds of *Enteromorpha intestinalis* and also high up on the shore may be the sea lettuce, *Ulva lactuca*. Then come the brown algae, all firmly attached: first the chanelled wrack, *Pelvetia canaliculata*, able to remain dry for long periods, followed by flat wrack, *Fucus spiralis*, bladder wrack, *Fucus vesiculosus*, and knotted wrack, *Ascophylum nodosum* and finally toothed wrack, *Fucus serratus*, still lower down.

Uncovered at the lowest tides and extending out beyond are the thong weed, *Himanthalea lorea*, and the stout-stemmed, large-fronded, tangle weeds, *Laminaria digitata* and *L. saccarina*.

The numerous species of red algae are smaller, often of delicate habit, and are generally attached in sheltered situations, often to the stems of wracks and tangles. A common one is *Chondrus crispus*.

STONEY SHORES

Suppose now that you are walking down on to a shore of stones and boulders at low tide, for example around Ardgartan. First to be seen is the drift-line of dead weed and debris at the limit of the sea's advance. Disturb this and scores of "hoppers", amphipod crustaceans of the genus *Orchestia*, spring into the air, while, concealed in the debris, may be found the nocturnal isopod, the sea slater, *Ligia oceanica*. Both are scavengers of decaying matter like most of their order.

From the upper tidal level down to low water the whole shore is encrusted with a carpet of the little white cones of acorn barnacles firmly cemented to stones and the shells of the also abundant mussels, *Mytilus edulis*. Despite the molluscan appearance of its conical shell, the acorn barnacle is a crustacean. It has sacrificed freedom of movement for the safety of sessile life. Concealed within the shell when exposed, it becomes active when submerged. Putting forth hair-fringed legs through the apical opening of the shell, it wafts minute particles of food to its mouth. Like so many of the shore animals, the barnacle starts life in the plankton. Eggs are shed into the sea and the ensuing free-swimming larvae pass through a series of (nauplius) stages to one, the "cypris" stage, which sinks to the bottom, selects a site, cements itself head down by means of glands in the antennae and develops the surrounding shell: thereafter being fixed for the rest of its life.

The common mussel, *Mytilus edulis* and the larger horse mussel, *Modiolus modiolus*, which lives in the Laminaria zone, hold fast by a bunch of threads (the byssus). As all bivalves do, they obtain microscopic food by filtration through the fine sieves of their gill plates. They too start life in the plankton, swimming by means of a cilia-encircled disc above the valves of the tiny shell.

With barnacles and mussels, a third fixed animal decorates smooth-surfaced stones, shells and seaweeds with tiny white, calcified tubes, cemented in flat spirals to their supports. This is an annelid worm, *Spirorbis borealis*, one of the successful and almost exclusively marine class of segmented worms, the Polychaeta. Immerse it in seawater and it protrudes brightly coloured, pinnate, tentacles, fringed with bristles, with which to collect its food. Lower down the shore is a similar but larger species *Pomatoceros triqueter*.

Equally abundant is the common periwinkle, *Littorina littorea*, free to move, of course, but protected from drying and mechanical damage by a lid (operculum) borne on the foot and closing the shell when the animal retracts into it. Species of this genus of marine snails show increasing adaptation of life out of water. Indeed, as has been observed, they may be used as an illustration of evolution to terrestrial life. The small periwinkle, *Littorina neritoides*, living so far up that it may only be submerged at the height of spring tides, has what is functionally a lung and can breathe air. The rough periwinkle, *Littorina rudis*, also living high up the shore, can breathe air but has a reduced gill; while *L. littorea*, living lower down the shore, has normal gills.

Studding the boulders are the conical shells of the common limpet, *Patella vulgata*, a gastropod mollusc which has relinquished the predominant spiral form in favour of a wide-based cone and allowed the development of an almost circular foot with the property of powerful adhesion. From a chosen spot on which to stay when uncovered it browses over the rock for short distances during immersion and returns again to exactly the same spot. Indeed it may grind a groove there for better contact to seal in water round its gills during exposure.

51

All gastropods gain their food with a radula, a strip of tissue beset with minute teeth, moving back and forth within the mouth and rasping like a strip of sandpaper. Limpets, periwinkles, top-shells (*Gibbula*) and others are vegetarian but occurring commonly with the common periwinkle is another gastropod, the dog whelk, *Nucula purpurea*, which is a carnivore and modified to that end by carrying the radula on a proboscis with which to bore through the shells of other molluscs and reach its prey.

In the common periwinkle and the dog whelk larval planktonic life has been superseded by attachment of eggs and advancement to a stage resembling the adult before hatching. The flask-shaped egg cases of the dog whelk are frequent in the next habitat to be examined: the humid microcosm of the weed-draped stones.

Turn back the weed and turn over stones (but, in the interest of conservation please return them) and you will find most of the kinds of animal frequenting this type of shore, both sessile and mobile. As you go down to the lower limit of the tide their number increases.

Prominent on stones is the beadlet sea anemone, *Actinia equina*, contracted to a red mass until immersed when it expands to all its flower-like beauty of column and crown of tentacles around its mouth. Likewise a grey-white, somewhat spherical, papillated, body in the same situation reveals nothing of its identity. Place it in a vessel of seawater and it expands to reveal itself as a sea slug, one of the nudibranch molluscs. It may prove to be either the sea lemon, *Acanthodoris pilosa*, or the common grey sea slug, *Aeolidia papillosa*, which feeds on the sea anemones. The first has an ovoid body carrying a pair of slender tentacles and gills standing up from the hind end of its back in the form of a crown of fringed rays. The second is more elongate, carries two pairs of tentacles, is without the crown of rays and has more pronounced papillae.

Equally prominent, if only because of their size and colour, are the familiar echinoderms, the common starfish, *Asterias rubens*, and a sea urchin, *Psammechinus miliaris*. The echinoderms are unique in the construction and organisation of their bodies. To hold on to solid supports and move slowly about them they have what may well be termed a hydraulic system operating a multitude of "tube-feet"; slender tubes terminating in suckers. Of these there are two rows along each of the starfishes five arms and similar double rows along five longitudinal bands on the globular sea urchin. Moving over the rocks, sea urchins browse on encrusting organisms. For this purpose they are equipped with a complex skeletal structure (known as "Aristotle's lantern") which protrudes five chisel teeth through the mouth.

The entirely carnivorous starfish, on the other hand, has no such teeth and a small mouth also. It attacks a bivalve, say a mussel, by attaching the tube-feet of opposite arms to the two halves of the shell; then slowly but relentlessly pulls until the shell is forced open. Its next problem is how to ingest the mussel with a mouth too small to engulf it. It overcomes this by everting its stomach over the prey and digesting that to a state that can be swallowed.

Again life starts for an echinoderm in the plankton as a transparent larva about one-twentieth of an inch long, its body drawn out into slender arms bearing the cilia with which it swims and looking totally unlike the armoured radial animal it eventually becomes.

Less obvious because their colour tends to match their background are two molluscs: tortoiseshell limpets of the genus, *Acmaea*, smaller and with a lower cone than the common limpet, and chitons or coat-of-mail shells having oval shells of eight articulating plates enabling them to roll up like armadillos when disturbed. Of these the common species are *Lepidochiton cinerius* and *Tonicella rubra*.

Capturing their food by means of tentacles, not sieving it from the water, are more sessile animals on the overhangs of boulders or on the holdfasts and fronds of seaweeds low down on the shore where there is no risk of drying.

A lens will show that a spreading "fur" of whitish threads is a colony of *Obelia* or other hydroid coelenterate relatives of the sea anemones, whose branches bear tentacled feeding polyps and little receptacles liberating swimming-bells (medusae) which are the planktonic sexual phase of the animal's life cycle. Their enormously larger cousins, the jellyfishes of which *Aurelia aureta* and *Rhizostoma octopus* are to be seen pulsing slowly in the sea or cast up dead on shore, likewise have a minute hydroid stage.

Higher up the scale of bodily construction are the moss-animalcules or Polyzoa. When magnified, the grey-white encrusting film spreading over *Laminaria* fronds proves to be a delicate lace-like tracery of rectangular chambers each containing a tentacular polyp of a colony of *Membranipora membranacea*.

Then there are sessile animals of similar habit, in that they filter water for their food, but are of widely different groups. Encrusting are sponges, the simplest of multicellular animals. The commonest are the bread-crumb sponge, *Halichondria panicea* and purse sponges of the genus *Leucosolenia*.

A small bivalve, *Saxicava arctica*, holding on by byssus threads, nestles in crevices and feeds in the manner described. A third type much higher up the evolutionary scale, for they are considered to be the forerunners of vertebrate animals, are the protochordate sea squirts. The solitary whitish flask of *Ciona intestinalis*, hangs down from boulders or the often beautifully coloured, compound, star sea squirts, *Botryllus schlosseri* and *Botrylloides leachi,* encrust them.

Sea squirts filter food from the water by means of a sieve formed by the finely perforated fore part of the alimentary canal and their larvae join the plankton as tailed "tadpoles", a name suggested by their resemblance to the tadpole of a frog.

As weed is moved aside or a stone turned over, your attention is probably first claimed by the more active animals, especially the ubiquitous shore crab, *Carcinus maenas,* either scuttling for cover or striking a defensive pose with upraised claws.

Hardy and wide in its range, this supreme scavenger is familiar to all who have been on a sea beach. Less well known is that its active life commences in the plankton, although the eggs are carried between abdomen and carapace by the female for protection. The first stage, larva (zoea), looking rather like a shrimp with a spine on its back, is followed by a stage (megalopa), crab-like in appearance but with the abdomen still extended and not folded under the carapace as in the adult.

Very active too is a fish, the butterfish or gunnel, *Centrotus gunellus,* skipping away as a stone is turned and recognisable by ten or twelve large black spots along the back of the laterally flattened, eel-like, body. Laying eggs in hollows and crevices, both parents guard them until hatched but the young spend a period in the plankton before taking to bottom life on the shore.

Between a stone and the wet sand or gravel on which it rests is a habitat occupied by worms. The nemertine worms have segmented, smooth, soft, featureless bodies and, although they are slow-moving helpless looking animals, they are carnivorous. They capture their prey by suddenly everting a long proboscis having a sticky glandular surface, armed also in some species with a piercing stylet and poison glands. A white species, *Amphiporus lactifloreus,* is only one to three inches in length but, should the black-brown bootlace worm, *Lineus longissimus,* be found, it is enormously long. It is not unusual to find one reaching a length of fifteen feet, lying intertwined beneath a stone. Life again begins in the plankton, this time as a minute larva (a pilidium) shaped like a helmet with two side flaps hanging down and a tuft of long cilia rising from the top.

Of more likely occurrence are members of the Polychaeta, the worms bearing bristles in lobes along their sides. One to be found here is the scale worm, *Lepidonotus squamatus,* so named because of the double row of overlapping scales over its back.

ROCK POOLS

In the rock pools of Strone may be found all the animals so far referred to, together with others. Here exposure is no longer a hazard though temperature changes during the day remain. Being in natural aquaria, animals inhabiting them can be seen behaving as those of the exposed shore do when the tide is in.

A miniature forest of red weeds, *Chondrus* and *Gigartina*, gives shade and concealment and wandering through it or swimming freely is the aesop prawn, *Pandalus montagui*, peculiar to pools. Resting on the bottom but darting into the weed when disturbed is a fish additional to the gunnel. This is the sea scorpion, *Cottus scorpius*, recognisable by its broad and spiny head.

Some of the abundant whelk and periwinkle shells can be seen to move about quickly and are then found to house a hermit crab, *Eupagurus bernhardi*. Present also on the exposed shore, hermit crabs are not readily noted because they are all withdrawn into their shells. The soft asymmetrical abdomen fits the spiral of the shell and is held in by a terminal appendage while the right nipper is much larger than the left to act as a cover to the shell opening on retraction.

SAND SHORES

Compared to the rocky shores we have seen, the sand shore has little to show when the tide is out for its denizens are burrowers, going down to levels below the risks of drying or of rapidly changing temperature.

Spiral castings of sand and a depression near by each denote the U-shaped burrows of the lugworm, *Arenicola marina*, so well known to all sea anglers as a bait. The lugworm is a polychaete adapted for a life of swallowing sand, as an earthworm does earth, and extracting nourishment from any organic matter it contains but, unlike an earthworm, *Arenicola* does not move about much. It behaves in such a way as to cause fresh sand to fall down that arm of the U which is indicated by the depression and provide it with a continual supply of food. Carnivorous or omnivorous polychaetes of the genus *Nereis* or allied genera, inhabiting the sand, also burrow as do the bivalve molluscs of which there are numerous sand gapers, *Mya arenaria* and common cockles, *Cardium edule*. But, all these animals can only be found by energetic digging except for the cockle. The cockle being able to swim by flapping the valves of its shell, is sometimes to be seen lying on the surface, having been left by the tide on a gravelly area, unsuitable for burrowing.

ESTUARIES

The last littoral environment to be considered is that of the river estuaries where saltwater changes to fresh as you leave the sea. Here plants and animals must be able to live in water of varying salinity and not very many are.

Looking at the estuarine shores of the Rivers Echaig or Goil as the tide flows out, the green algae, *Enteromorpha* and *Ulva* are much in evidence beyond the *Fucus*. In clearings between weeds in the down-flowing water swim shoals of opossum shrimps, *Praunus flexuosus*, all facing head upstream. Amphipod shrimps of the genus *Gammarus* are likewise abundant under weed and stones both in and out of the water as indeed is the purely marine *Gammarus locusta* over all the shores but here *G. locusta* gives way to the brackish-water frequenting *G. zaddachi* and that to the purely freshwater species, *G. pulex* as their distribution is followed up the river. However, the three species are very similar in appearance and require detailed study for their identification.

Some species of fish are physiologically adjusted to survival in waters of changing salinity. The sand goby, *Gobius minutus*, extends its range up from the sea into the brackish estuary and the three-spined stickleback, *Gasterosteus aculeatus*, extends down from freshwater. Flounders, *Pleuronectes flesus*, may pass right up into freshwater to feed and, as is well known, salmon and sea trout pass through to breed in streams, while young eels, *Anguilla anguilla*, end their long migration to live in freshwater until maturity dictates their return to the Sargasso Sea to breed.

PELAGIC FISHES

Sea anglers will perhaps wonder why fish of commerce and sport have not been at least listed, apart from those passing into or through the estuaries. For the most part they are those commonly found around our shores. Codling, haddock, whiting, saithe (coal-fish) and lythe (pollack) of the cod family: the seabed frequenting rather than pelagic flat fish, plaice and dab: mackerel in the summer months: skate and thorn-back ray may all afford sport for the visitor.

FRESHWATER LOCHS AND STREAMS

Lacking the permanence of the seas and being in close proximity to the land, freshwaters have a different and less diverse flora and fauna as a result of invasions from sea and land.

Such large algae as the seaweeds are not to be found. Flowering plants and a few rooted cryptogams (mosses and their allies) take their place but with less luxuriance. Some of the major groups of marine animals are either absent or poorly represented but others derived originally from the land, have come to occupy all available niches; predominantly the insects. Small and never spectacular the freshwater invertebrates need lenses of, say, X3 to X10 magnification for their recognition and then often show unsuspected beauty of form.

56

Plate 29. Shyest and brightest of the Park's birds, a kingfisher, *Alcedo atthis*, pauses from its search for minnows.

Plate 30. Adult swan, *Cygnus olor*, and young cygnet at Dornach Bay, Loch Eck.

Plate 31. A buzzard, *Buteo buteo*, a large ground-feeding hawk, pounces towards its prey.

Plate 32. The long-tailed field mouse, *Apodemus sylvaticus*, probably the most numerous mammal in the Forest Park.

Plate 33. Female hen harrier, *Circus cyaneus*, and nestlings. This ground-nesting hawk, which feeds largely on birds, has spread rapidly in recent years.

Plate 34. The ptarmigan, *Lagopus mutus*, a rare grouse found only on the highest peaks in the north of the Park, changes colour from white in winter to brown in summer. This bird shows intermediate spring plumage.

Plate 35. A shy roebuck, *Capreolus capreolus*, in summer, when its antlers are fully developed.

Plate 36. Red deer, *Cervus elephas*, females, called hinds, seen in winter in a young plantation of Norway spruce.

Plate 37.   A salmon pool in Glen Massan.

Plate 38.   A rock pool on the shore at Strone Point.

Plate 39. Lugworms in the sand at Kilmun. Beyond, across the Holy Loch, lies Sandbank.

Plate 40. The boulder-strewn shore of Loch Goil; note seaweeds.

Plate 41. Atlantic grey seal, *Halichoerus grypus*.

Plate 42. The rare Loch Lomond powan, *Coregonus lavaretus clupeoides*, found also in Loch Eck.

Plate 43. Life on a sea-shore boulder; knotted wrack, beadlet anemones, limpets and periwinkles

Plate 44. Acorn barnacles.

Seawater is rich in the inorganic salts which all green plants must have and it is constant in its composition whereas freshwaters have not only very much lower but widely variable concentrations of these nutrients. It follows therefore that the production of green plants, and consequently of animals, will be governed by the nutrient content of a particular water. The ancient Dalradian rocks of the Forest Park yield little of these salts to the water flowing over them and this purity of water is reflected in the lower production of life, in quantity and in kind, than in richer waters; rather more in the streams than in the lochs.

HILL STREAMS

To take running waters first, a good example is the stream flowing down Hell's Glen. Here shallow, fast flowing and stony-bedded riffles alternate with slower, deeper, pools. Vegetation is at a minimum, just a coating of microscopic algae, mainly diatoms on the stones, with mosses on some.

Lift out a stone and the larvae of insects scud across it, larvae of mayflies, caddisflies and stoneflies. Of the mayflies, *Baëtis*, with its stream-lined body, efficient claws and good power of swimming, may hold its own in the current over the stone. *Ecdyonurus* has a flattened body to occupy crevices underneath, where also will be the larvae of such stoneflies as *Leuctra*. Caddisflies are represented by the active and predacious larvae of *Rhyacophila* which have no enveloping case but build one fixed to the stone in which to pupate before emergence as the winged adult. Likewise caseless are the larvae of *Hydropsyche* and *Philopotamus* but these make a shelter of debris and spin a net before it to collect their food. The much larger larvae of such genera as *Stenophylax* and *Halesus* have mobile cylindrical cases of stone particles, heavy enough to aid their owners in avoiding being swept downstream, and *Goëra* improves the plain cylinder by weighting its case with additional larger pieces along the sides.

The use of the generic name only implies the presence or possible presence of several species. Anglers have common names for the adults of some mayflies and stoneflies and a few caddisflies but their larvae lack them.

LOCHS

Go now to a loch and there will be a greater range of habitats on the wave-cut littoral terrace bounding the main loch bed but now you are without the help of tides regularly uncovering them. Wading and the use of a hand net permits the study of shallows near to the margin but most of the terrace can only be dealt with by means of a boat and appropriate collecting gear.

Typical of Scottish lochs is a zonation of rooted plants down the slope of the terrace until water depth precludes sufficient light for them to exist; a zonation due to erosion and grading of the bed from stones through gravels and sands down to fine silts and mud.

Stones near the margin bear only tufts of the moss, *Fontinalis antepyretica*, for here turbulence engendered by onshore waves simulates the conditions of a hill stream. Beyond the stones, coarse sands are covered with a sward of shore weed or lakewort, *Littorella lacustris*, interspersed with water lobelia, *Lobelia dortmanna*, and millfoil, *Myriophylum spicatum*. Further out again where the sand is fining down to silt, *Litteorella* gives way to a sward of a plant very like it in appearance but which is a cryptogam, not a flowering plant. This is quillwort, *Isoëtes lacustris*. Finally comes a zone occupied by an upstanding alga, the stonewort, *Nitella opaca*.

The Loch Lomond boundary of the Park skirts the deep and narrow trough of the upper loch where the littoral terrace is not yet well developed, much of it consisting of a bed of unstable stones of little width before the steep descent to the great depths of the profundal floor, but this plant zonation can be seen at Tarbet. Loch Eck, though not so deep, is somewhat similar but a bay at Dornoch Point will serve here and also all of the small and shallower Loch Restil.

Animals living on the terrace tend to show a similar zonation as may be seen in Loch Lomond, taken here as an example because the other lochs still await detailed study. On the stones may be patches of a sponge, *Ephydatia*, the only sessile filter-feeder in freshwater, and over the stones glide planarian flatworms of the genera *Dendrocoelum*, *Dugesia* and *Polycelis*.

It is only in this turbulent zone that animals typical of hill streams find a suitable habitat: the mayfly, *Ecdyonurus*, the freshwater limpet, *Ancylus fluviatilis*, limpet-shaped but not a true limpet, and a small stone-cased caddis, *Agapetus fuscipes*, together with other stone-cased species. The wandering snail, *Limnaea pereger*, lays its eggs on stones but extends widely over the littoral to be joined in the deeper regions by the little gill-bearing gastropod, *Valvata piscinalis*. Freshwater shrimps, *Gammarus pulex*, swim among the stones and out over the next zone where also is an isopod, the freshwater slater, *Asellus aquaticus*. *Asellus*, being adapted to life on fine silts, ranges out beyond the limit of the littoral terrace.

These crustaceans and molluscs appear to be either absent or rare in Lochs Eck and Restil, probably due to an insufficiency of calcium which they require for the calcium content of Loch Lomond is 7.0 to 10.4, of Loch Eck 2.0, and Loch Restil 1.4 parts per million.

In the *Littorella* and *Isoëtes* zones we find a richer and more varied fauna. Our only burrowing mayfly larva, *Ephemera danica*, inhabits

58

the sand. *Centroptilum*, a form similar to *Baëtis*, and the weakly-swimming *Leptophlebia* browse on diatoms covering the rooted plants. Aquatic beetles and bugs, rising to the surface for air, keep to the shallower water. Caddises of a number of genera of which *Limnephilus*, *Lepidostoma* and *Phrygania* may be quoted as a series showing a range in the constitution of their larval cases from mixed sand grain and vegetable materials to purely the latter with their distribution tending to follow the increasing depth and placidity of the water: heavier cases inshore to lighter cases offshore. The deeper, calmer, water and finer bottom sediments are particularly suited to a tiny mayfly larva, *Caenis*, adapted for life on silts and here the populations build up of oligochaete worms (there are no freshwater polychaetes), related to and behaving like earthworms, particularly of the genera *Lumbriculus* and *Tubifex*; the isopod *Asellus* together with the little bivalve peashells, *Sphaerium* and *Pisidium* and a leech, *Helobdella stagnalis*.

The worms, the leech and *Pisidium* range out on to the muds of the main profundal bed. Joined by larvae of the non-biting midge family, the Chironomidae, they form the bulk of the fauna there.

The chironomids have not so far been mentioned because these small insects are very difficult and often impossible to identify to species, even sometimes to genera, at our present state of knowledge; even by an expert in their study. They are the most successful of the insect families for they have exploited every kind of habitat in loch and stream. Some swimming freely, others burrowing or occupying attached or free "houses", they feed on microscopic organisms, decaying debris or are predaceous on other equally small animals.

FISHES

In conclusion, mention must be made of the fishes for there are two fish of especial note.

These are the powan, *Coregonus lavaretus clupeoides*, and a char, *Salvelinus alpinus youngeri*. They are sub-species to be found nowhere else. The powan is in Lochs Lomond and Eck, the char only in Loch Eck; although they have close relatives in lakes around the northern hemisphere. Some ten thousand years ago at the end of the Ice Age, these fish are thought to have been marine and entered freshwaters to spawn as salmon do today, but that some evolved into entirely freshwater populations and were subsequently isolated when the land rose after the ice retreated.

This past history of the powan still governs its reproduction. Although the adult fish roam over all the loch throughout the year and experience summer temperatures around 60° Fahrenheit, exposure of their eggs to 50° kills them in a few hours. Spawning takes place in winter, mostly through the month of January. The eggs are scattered at random on gravel beds where silt will not accumulate to smother them. There they lie for some twelve weeks before hatching and are preyed upon not only by other fishes but by powan themselves, also by an unusual predator on fish eggs, the larva of our largest caddisfly, *Phrygania*.

The powan abounds and its abundance can be explained by its manner of feeding. Whereas the other fishes feed on the bottom animals of the littoral terraces (or upon each other) and have about ten per cent of the area of the loch in which to find them, the powan are not so restricted for they feed on the vast number of minute crustacea of the plankton present over the whole of the loch.

Unless it is the fish called a "Goldie" in the *New Statistical Account of Scotland* of 1845, and it probably is, the char was unknown in Loch Eck until twenty years ago. Strange as this may seem, it may well be because it lives out in the deep water feeding on plankton as does the powan and has not fallen a victim to the lure of an angler.

Of other species, Loch Lomond has fourteen including all three species of lampreys, the cyclostomes or jaw-less fishes. Their distribution is not yet fully understood but not all of them extend to the upper loch. Those to be expected are salmon, trout (both sea trout and brown trout), perch, three-spined stickleback, and eel. Loch Eck has these but lacks the perch, while Loch Restil has trout.

Heron

60

BIBLIOGRAPHY

HARDY, ALISTER C.   1956: *The Open Sea.* The New Naturalist. Collins, London.

BARRETT, JOHN and YONGE, C. M.   1958: *Collins Pocket Guide to the Sea Shore.* Collins, London.

MACAN, T. T. and WORTHINGTON, E. B.   1951: *Life in Lakes and Rivers.* The New Naturalist. Collins, London.

TIPPETT, R.   1974: *A Natural History of Loch Lomond.* Glasgow University Press.

YONGE, C. M.   1949: *The Sea Shore.* The New Naturalist. Collins, London.

I am not the first to have imagined forests returning.

—Robin Fulton.

FORESTRY

BY A. G. BRAMWELL

THE BACKGROUND

THE chapter on Plant Life lists the kinds of trees that occur naturally in the Park. The present areas of natural woodland are small, however, being mainly confined to the lower slopes and valley bottoms. From evidence unearthed in upland peat bogs it is certain that these woodlands were much more extensive in olden days and composed of oak, hazel, ash and alder, with a proportion of birch increasing with altitude until the upper fringes were almost pure birch.

It was recorded in the first *Statistical Account of Scotland* for the parish of Lochgoilhead and Kilmorich that "In all the mosses in this country, even in those on the tops of the hills, stumps of trees of various kinds are found and there is no doubt that this country was much covered in timber." It is probable that the upper limits of the oakwood were at about 250 metres and the birch woods would extend to some 350 metres above sea level.

Prior to the mid-eighteenth century the area was farmed by crofters, mainly living in small lowland townships but having their mountain shielings for summer grazing. Though oats, barley and latterly, potatoes were grown for subsistence the climate and soils were not suitable for arable farming. Grazing of black cattle, horses and folded sheep around the shielings contributed to the thinning out of the upland forests as did the demand for fuel. Extensive areas were utilised as deer forests for hunting.

During the eighteenth century and the first half of the nineteenth these natural woodlands were cut for charcoal for smelting and tan bark. At first iron ore was transported by pack horse to small charcoal bloomeries, traces of which can be seen on many hillsides. No attempt was made to regenerate the felled woodlands.

In 1754 smelting works were opened at Furnace and the intake of timber involved the felling of some 48 hectares of woodland each year. The scale of this market led to management of oak woodlands for continuous yield on a twenty-year felling cycle. From the stumps of the trees, young shoots spring up and these were protected from stock for the first seven years, reduced to two or three stems in thinning operations and finally clear felled on maturity. This system, known as coppicing, was widely used in the area, more especially at Arrochar, Lochgoilhead, Glenshellish and Glenfinart.

Generations of foresters practised their skill in this way until the use of charcoal for smelting was superseded by coal, leaving tan bark and gun powder charcoal as the main woodland products. Finally, by 1880, even these had been undercut by cheaper foreign imports, with the result that the woodlands were neglected and the local timber industry fell into a decline.

These early efforts at management concerned mainly the oakwoods but over much the same period the traditional methods of farming were swept away by a tide of reform involving clearance of the crofters together with considerable areas of the higher lying forest to make way for the open grazings for black face sheep. The system spread engulfing woods and deer forests until by 1790 it was recorded in the first *Statistical Account of Scotland* that ". . . the hills are gradually growing green since the sheep flocks have been introduced; the heath is decaying fast wherever the sheep are allowed to pasture." In this way sheep farming became the major land use in the forest park area.

The eighteenth century also saw the beginnings of the movement towards plantations of conifer species, brought from all over the world by landowners who vied with one another to increase the range of their collections. The area of the Park was little affected by this movement but there are records of square miles of mature plantations at Inveraray by 1785 and of extensive areas of Scots pine, larch, silver fir, beeches and other hardwoods at Ardkinglas.

63

It is also recorded that some 1,000 acres of conifers had been planted at Luss between 1779 and 1794 and it is evident that the landscape must already have been assuming some aspects of its present character.

Within the Park various estate owners adorned their policy woodlands with the exotic species some of which are now planted in large numbers and they thus performed a valuable pioneering role in the later establishment of the large present day forests in the area.

Prominent among these was David Napier the engineer who built the first steamship *Comet* and who held Glenshellish farm from 1826–1870. Some very well grown specimens of his plantings of Douglas fir, Scots pine, Sitka and Norway spruces and larch can still be seen near Glenbranter Forest Office.

In 1871 John Duncan of Benmore planted the famous Giant Redwood avenue and Arboretum which are a notable feature of the Botanical Gardens, together with the magnificent stands of Douglas fir, Sitka spruce and larch on Cruach Hill, which date from 1879.

From 1800 to 1862 the Earls Dunsmore planted similar species around the mansion house at Glenfinart.

The Forestry Commission was formed in 1919 and its first acquisition in Scotland was of Glenbranter Estate where 10,000 acres were purchased from Sir Harry Lauder in 1921. Between the wars during a period of agricultural depression acquisition of land proceeded rapidly, continuing at a slower pace after 1946 until by 1974 the extent of forest land in the Park was in round figures as follows:

Acres (1 acre—0.405 hectare)

	Plantations and plantable land	Agricultural and other land (mainly mountainsides)	Total area
Ardgartan Forest	12,600	19,500	32,100
Benmore Forest (part)	7,400	10,600	18,000
Glenbranter Forest (part)	8,400	7,200	15,600
Forest Park (totals)	28,400	37,300	65,700

The Park thus contains 103 square miles of rugged country deeply intersected by sea and fresh water lochs, with public roads skirting the periphery of the main mountain massifs and providing adequate access for day visitors wishing to picnic, fish, pony trek or launch their boats. For the more adventurous walkers or climbers the forest roads and tracks reach far into the hinterland where they can enjoy the solitude of forest and mountain wilderness.

The chapter on Geology describes the processes which gave the

Park its mountainous, fiord-like character. Superimposed over this are the effects of glaciation, mainly the deposition of clay, sand and gravel mixed with boulders, which cover a large part of the area.

The more fertile lower slopes consist of brown forest soils while on the intermediate slopes the gravelly morainic mounds protrude from a matrix of poorly drained mineral soils finally merging into the hill peats and skeletal soils of the upper slopes up to the tree planting limits. In this locality, with rainfall averaging 100 inches per annum and with the prevailing strong winds, tree limits for conifers vary from 350 to 400 metres above sea level, depending on exposure and soil.

When land is acquired for forestry, it generally includes a proportion of unplantable ground, but care is taken to reserve the low lying arable fields for agricultural use in conjunction with the higher grazing ground. In this way, apart from the most barren hill tops and a few small areas not worth enclosing, the whole of the Park is under productive, integrated land use.

The proportions of plantable soils are as follows:

Well drained mineral soils	26%	Brown earths and Ironpan soils
Poorly drained mineral soils with shallow peat	61%	Gleyed soils
Deep peats	9%	Hill peats and bogs
Skeletal soils	4%	

Harvesting tanbark and burning charcoal—*circa 1850*

65

Recognition of these different soil types and their characteristic vegetation is important to the forester as each has its own special requirement for cultivation, drainage and fertiliser treatment.

To maintain and harvest the plantations the Commission currently employs about 80 forest workers and 20 contractors, supported by 20 road and mechanical engineers. Much of the harvesting is carried out by timber merchants who employ 40 men, to give a total of 160 men and women earning their livelihood in the forest. Further ramifications of the industry are difficult to quantify, but in addition to supplying pulpwood to Fort William and logs and pit-props to English markets two local wood-processing industries employ some 41 men and haulage of timber from forest to mills occupies a further 20 men.

To accommodate its own supervisors and directly employed workers the Commission maintains no less than 114 houses in the Park.

CREATING THE FORESTS

FORMATION OF NEW PLANTATIONS

While the fertile, well drained mineral soils allow a wide variety of conifers to be grown nearly three-quarters of the plantable ground is covered with peat of varying thickness which greatly restricts the choice of species.

The main coniferous species used in the forests are spruces, both Sitka and Norway spruce, Lodgepole pine and Scots pine and three species of larch (European, Japanese and a hybrid of these two) are also planted. In addition there are small proportions of Douglas fir, Silver fir, Lawson cypress, Western hemlock and Western red cedar. Each species is planted in the situation to which it is best adapted and the forester uses the natural ground vegetation as one of his guides to deciding which to plant.

Spruces are planted in moister places notably on peats and where rushes tend to grow. Larches require well drained soils often characterised by bracken, and pines are reserved for the sites where heather is dominant.

In earlier days when cultivation and drainage was done by hand, choice of species closely followed these principles and many fine mature stands in the Park are a testimony to the forester's skill. Nowadays cultivation and draining ploughs and the ability to distribute fertilisers in large quantities from aircraft have enabled us to ameliorate site conditions and hence we find Sitka spruce, the hardiest and most productive tree in our conditions, being planted much more extensively.

Broadleaved trees have not been grown on any scale, though some beech, red oak and sycamore have been established along public roads for amenity purposes.

Currently the proportion of tree species forming our plantations is as follows:

Spruces	81%
Larches	8%
Pines	6%
Other Conifers	5%

The trees are raised in nurseries in the eastern parts of the country where the rainfall is much lower; they are usually 2–3 years old and about 10 inches tall when planted out. On the hill the trees are planted fairly closely together at espacements varying according to the soil and exposure; on average about 800 trees to the hectare.

For those readers who are interested in the botanical description and other properties of the tree species mentioned above there are two well illustrated Forestry Commission publications published by H.M.S.O.:

Booklet No. 15	*Know your Conifers*	(price, 1975, 30p)
Booklet No. 18	*Know your Hardwoods*	(price, 1975, £1)

As in agriculture the objectives in cultivating forest soils are to provide a favourable planting medium by improving local drainage, loosening the soil and releasing its nutrients and to suppress weed growth by turning over large furrows.

On the well drained brown earths, cultivation is necessary to prevent the young trees from being suppressed by strong growth of grasses and bracken. With ironpan soils cultivation shatters the pan layer which is impenetrable to the tree roots and releases the nutrients locked up at lower levels. On the stiff gleyed soils improved local drainage is the main aim, while on the mainly shallow peats the result of cultivation is to bring to the surface the underlying mineral soils and so release their nutrients.

All cultivation is carried out up and down the slopes but on the steepest hills, where tractors cannot go and erosion is likely, it is necessary to revert to expensive hand cutting of turves.

Within five years of cultivation a complete system of deep drainage ditches is superimposed across the furrows, laid out as near to the contours as possible, in order to remove the surface water in this high rainfall area. By reducing the length of run-off down the furrows these drains also check erosion.

Tree roots cannot penetrate into saturated soil and the formation of a deep drainage system enhances the stability of the crops. Shallow rooted trees may blow down at a very early age on exposed sites so good drainage is very important.

Despite such precautions once or twice in a century there occur storms of such force that no tree crops can stand in their path. The hurricane of 1968 levelled some 4,000 acres of forest in the Park equivalent to five years of normal production at that time. It took three years of intensive effort to clear and market the timber. The effects of this storm on the landscape have been quite dramatic but clearly indicate that large areas of forest can be removed without detriment to amenity providing no attempts are made to tidy and straighten edges and remove substantial remnants.

On the more fertile ground and in bracken patches it is necessary to cut the competing weeds back from the young trees. Formerly this weeding would be done entirely by hand, using sickles. Nowadays an increasingly amount of weeding is carried out by very careful application of selective weed killers.

Prior to the 1968 hurricane virtually all planting was on bare ground long denuded of tree crops. As the windblown areas were cleared the ground was quickly replanted.

Young trees planted in the felling debris are vulnerable to harmful beetles and are dipped in an insecticide before planting. With the creation of forest soil conditions there is less need to cultivate the soil when replanting but the opportunity is taken to improve the drainage system by mechanical diggers.

The experience gained from the windblow was put to good use in the development of techniques in restocking the ground following normal harvesting of mature stands. Forests are a rare example of a perpetually renewable natural resource.

PROTECTION OF THE PLANTATIONS

In the early years trees are vulnerable to browsing damage from domestic stock and rabbits, voles, roe and red deer.

Rabbits in this area of high rainfall, though present on the drier slopes, never presented any great problems and since the myxomatosis outbreaks of the 1950s have ceased to be a significant factor.

Throughout the area and particularly in Glenbranter from 1930 to 1933 there was a vole plague which literally decimated the earlier plantings in Glenshellish. It is recorded that "the plague was so severe that walking over the hill one could not avoid tramping on mice. Men at lunchtime could feed the creatures on bread, if they had not stolen it before; mice ate the plants before the eyes of men who had planted them so that complete replacement was necessary." After reaching its height in 1932 the plague gradually died out and since that time there have only been local outbreaks.

While nothing can be done to cope with population explosions of this order control of deer is effected, not by fencing them out which would be very expensive, but by systematic culling in vulnerable plantations. The aim is to maintain stocks at a level where the damage to young plantations is acceptable, the presence of these creatures in the Park being regarded as an asset to be preserved. For the control of deer seven skilled Rangers are employed. The venison is sold to markets as far afield as West Germany and yields a worthwhile revenue which is a secondary reason for exercising planned control.

To protect our trees from sheep and cattle and indeed to safeguard stock from injury in deeply cultivated ground it is necessary to maintain stock fences round the periphery of our forest blocks. In deciding on fence lines there is full consultation with neighbouring farmers to ensure adequate access to upland grazings and to guard against the formation of "sheep traps" in broken country. Fences which traverse streams, gullies and the highest hills are subjected to damage from floods, snow and landslides and require regular inspection by our Rangers and maintenance to keep them secure.

The damage caused over the seasons by wild life is nothing to the devastation which can be caused by man in a few hours. In the period January–June the dead ground vegetation, especially grass and bracken, will ignite easily on a dry sunny day if a visitor is careless with matches, cigarettes, picnic stoves, etc. A major outbreak of fire can build up rapidly under these conditions. To avoid this, visitors are requested to protect their forests by:

Reporting any outbreak of fire to the fire brigade.

Using the fire brooms or beaters to put out ground fires.

Trying to persuade less thoughtful visitors to discontinue dangerous practices.

Parking vehicles so as to prevent obstructions to fire-vehicles at forest entrances.

Giving way to fire-fighting vehicles.

HARVESTING AND MARKETING TIMBER

When first planted trees are fairly closely spaced to suppress the competing ground vegetation and to ensure adequate stocking in spite of natural losses and in time their branches intermingle to form a dense thicket. Unless the crop is opened out too many trees will be either suppressed or unable to increase in girth at a steady rate. This opening out, or "thinning" is designed to give the best formed and most vigorous trees just enough space to keep growing at the optimum rate. Too drastic an opening would encourage development of heavy side branches and produce poor, knotty timber. At this stage the trees are still small and not very valuable and the forester times his first thinning as a compromise between the growth requirements of the crop and the need to cover the cost of the operation. As a rough rule thinning is begun when the tallest trees attain an average height of 40 feet.

Generally speaking thinning is started between the ages of 25–30 years and is repeated every five years thereafter until the crop is felled at about 50–60 years of age, depending on site and species.

Before thinning can start the forest road system must be designed and established to accommodate heavy timber traffic and suit the most appropriate method of extracting logs from stump to roadside. In dry, level country with hard mineral soil, wheeled skidding tractors can penetrate well into the wood and roads can be spaced far apart. In wet conditions with slippery peat and clay soils the practice is to extract timber by winches and cable ways with a maximum range of 600 metres. Depending on the difficulty of the terrain our roads can thus be spaced some 1,200 metres apart. As the forests in the Park are relatively old much of the road system was designed for horse extraction up to 120 metres and the roads are therefore closer together than in the younger areas.

As with all road transport timber lorries have tended to become longer and heavier over the years requiring stronger bearing surfaces, easier gradients and wider bends. Construction of roads is carried out by the Commission's own engineers, using standard techniques and modern earth moving machinery, but employing their own special expertise to surmount the peculiar difficulties of the terrain. Within the Park there are no less than 270 kilometres of timber roads which in themselves represent a considerable engineering achievement and as a bonus provide access to remote grazings for tenant farmers as well as miles of delightful walking for the tourist.

In thinning areas it will be noticed that the trees to be taken out have been blazed by skilled markers who will have sampled the volume being removed, controlling this according to the productive capacity of the stand. These markers also align "racks" at intervals alongside the roadside to allow the winch cables to be rigged for extraction.

The next stage is thinning by chainsaw operators who fell the racks and the blazed trees. Each feller is equipped with a light fast cutting saw, a belt carrying tools and retractable measuring tape and with other equipment for the treatment of stumps against fungal infection. After felling the tree is trimmed of its side branches, topped and cross cut into sawlogs and pulpwood stacked ready for extraction.

Behind the fellers the extraction team operates with tractor mounted winch. From its high tower the working cables reach into the wood to where the chokerman hitches on the loads of timber. Communication between the tractorman and chokerman is either by hand signals or radio if visibility is obstructed. At the roadside the winchman stacks the pulpwood and logs separately and neatly, ready for uplifting.

Lorries are loaded mechanically, by hydraulic grab. Timber is sold at the roadside either in short lengths of slender billets for the pulpmill at Fort William or medium diameter lengths for pitprops, pallet boards for fork lift trucks, chip board, wood wool, etc. The longer logs are sold to sawmills for conversion into building timber.

While visitors are welcome to watch the men at work from a safe distance, it is well to remember that when engines are running they cannot hear your approach. Please keep well out of the way of moving timber and ropes and your children and dogs under control and if a wide diversion is difficult don't attempt to pass an operator until he has seen you and signalled that it is safe to proceed.

LANDSCAPE AND RECREATION

SCENERY

Mention has already been made of the characteristic woodland landscape of the Park yet the greater part of it is still open grassland and mountain crag where ground vegetation is constantly changing colour with the seasons from the greenness of high summer to the warm purple of heather patches in August merging into the russet browns of the bracken and grasses in autumn. In winter when snow caps the peaks all the colours are highlighted and the mountains appear to take on a new dimension.

In more sharply undulating country the boundaries between forest and green hill are not usually obtrusive. In the Park with its steep, even slopes virtually the whole extent of the conifer plantations is in full view and the forest boundaries sometimes are out of harmony with the natural flowing lines of the hillsides. Currently much attention is being given to this aspect and to forest landscaping generally. As the opportunity arises steps are taken to achieve a degree of merging by leaving areas on the margins unplanted and by establishing various species, notably larch, in irregular drifts.

In addition to this, as the relatively uniform crops are broken by felling and windblow a mosaic of age classes will gradually develop to provide a much more natural appearance which will be further enhanced by leaving open features such as crags, streams and waterfalls. Wherever broadleaved stands occur these will be preserved in the interests of amenity and wildlife.

ENJOYING THE PARK

The wild and romantic scenery of the Park has long made it a favourite playground for the townsfolk of the West of Scotland. In

1905 Mr. Cameron Corbett, M.P., gifted his Ardgoil Estate, 15,000 acres, to the City of Glasgow for the recreational use of its people; by 1907 plans had been put forward for the afforestation of large tracts of land in the peninsula and for the construction of overland tracks for the benefit of the tourist. Though the forests were planted from 1918 onwards very little was done about the tracks but nevertheless day-trippers could travel by railway to Arrochar, by a multiplicity of steam packet companies and latterly by frequent bus services. The serious walker or climber could traverse overland routes assured of meeting homeward bound transport at his destination.

Nowadays, despite the virtual cessation of public transport services which reduced the usage of the Park for a time, more general car ownership has resulted in renewed pressure. This the Commission welcomes, while recognising the need for more facilities such as picnic sites, walks, etc. and for control to ensure that interests do not clash and most important of all that the environment does not suffer through indiscriminate or excessive use.

In addition to the normal day visitor and holidaymaker the area is used increasingly by pupils from urban schools attending courses at the five Outdoor Centres based in and around the Park. Each year some 5,000 children are introduced to country pursuits such as nature study, orienteering, back packing, camping, sailing and canoeing. They are versed in the Country Code and above all expert instructors ensure that they can enjoy these activities in safety and with consideration for others.

The mountain range to the north of the Arrochar to Inveraray road is a regular haunt of the rock climber and hill walker and this area is perhaps the most intensively used in all seasons.

The forest roads offer wide scope for peaceful walking and pony trekking and on strictly controlled occasions are used by Car Rally Clubs who are dependant on this facility for their sport.

Many famous infantry regiments and marine commando units carry out endurance exercises in the hills and this is perhaps the time to strike a note of warning. Too often family parties set off into the hills on a sunny morning, wearing elegant footwear and flimsy clothing, without map or compass and little else but boundless optimism. The visitor should know that the hills and climate are treacherous, visibility can be reduced to nil and temperatures drop very quickly. Even minor injuries can ruin a holiday and major ones a life. Please come prepared for hill walking with stout footwear and good warm rainproof clothing. Learn how to read a map and to use a compass. If you are not accustomed to strenuous walking don't attempt too much to begin with. We do want you to enjoy yourselves!

Plate 45. An Aesop prawn (*left*) and a beadlet anemone from a rock pool.

Plate 46. Life on a sea-shore boulder; whelks, tube-worms, and a sea-squirt.

Plate 47.   Entrance to the Younger Botanic Gardens at Benmore. The drive runs through a
magnificent avenue of Californian wellingtonias, *Sequoiadendron giganteum*.

Plate 48.   Felling a well-grown mature Douglas fir with a power-saw.

Plate 49. Until recent times horses were the main method of transport for logs between the felling point and the roadside. Note the simple harness.

Plate 50. Overhead winches, carried by the tractor that supplies the power, are nowadays the standard method for hauling in logs. Rigging a skyline winch at Glenbranter.

Plate 51. A hydraulic grab loads pulpwood logs, destined for the big paper mill at Fort William, on to the bed of a lorry.

Plate 52. Loading large logs suitable for sawing into planks at the sawmill.

Plate 53. Establishing the forest on bare ground. This picture, taken about 1940, shows a network of drains with small trees, pale in colour, interspersed between them. This hillside, on the by-road from Ardentinny to Loch Eck (seen distant), is now clothed

Plate 54. A giant tanker moored in Loch Long opposite the Forest Park. From this point, near Finnart, the oil is pumped across Scotland to a refinery at Grangemouth on the Forth.

Plate 55. The shore road through Kilmun, looking north along the Holy Loch towards the mountains of the Park.

Plate 56.   A sunny beach at Dornach Bay, Loch Eck, close to Glenbranter.

Plate 57.   Riders beside Loch Goil, with a view across the water towards the Ardgoil hills.

The Forestry Commissioners have drawn up by-laws which apply to the Forest Park as well as to all their other forests, both to protect the forest and to enhance the visitor's enjoyment. An over-riding rule is that cars and motor cycles are not allowed into the forest unless specially authorised, as there must be some places where people can get away from traffic. Since this Guide was first published in 1938 there have been substantial changes both in forest practices and in the requirements from forests. It is quite likely that this edition will equally be overtaken by events and the visitor is thus welcome to discuss any aspect with Forestry Commission staff.

PINE

Beside the loch
small ferns
beyond the grass
the rhododendrons
then the great pine
topmost branches disposed like fanning wings
as if an eagle
were at that instant lighting on its tip.

—Tom Buchan

Loch Eck from the Whistlefield road

Crossing corries, crossing forests
Crossing valleys long and wild,
The fair white Mary still uphold me
The Shepherd Jesu be my shield.
　　　　　　—Ora Turais: *Prayer for Travelling.*

SEEING THE PARK BY ROAD
By Herbert L. Edlin

Most visitors to the Park will come either by boat from Gourock across the Clyde to Dunoon, or by road from Glasgow via Loch Lomond, Arrochar and Strachur—a wonderful day's run from Glasgow or even Edinburgh.

route 1. DUNOON TO GLEN MASSAN, KILMUN, STRONE, ARDENTINNY, LARACH PASS AND LOCH ECK (30 miles without diversions, 43 miles otherwise, circular)

Dunoon, an attractive and modernised seaside resort just south of the Forest Park, is the starting point for this run. Many, if not most, visitors will have come across the Clyde from Gourock by the frequent car-ferries. First, they must negotiate Dunoon's simple

74

one-way-traffic system. From the pier, take the northward road (right turn on leaving jetty), first up the main street, then right by John Street, then left on regaining the promenade, and so along the shores of the Clyde, through Kirn to Hunter's Quay.

The seaside road now bends east a little to follow the shores of the Holy Loch and away across the water the great sweep of the Benmore Forest plantations—dark spruce and pine with paler larches—may be seen climbing high up the steep flank of Kilmun Hill. Its highest point, Cnoc a Mhadaidh, pronounced "Knock-a-vaddy", meaning "Hillock of the Wolf", rises to 1,542 feet above the sea. The broken pattern of woodland above Kilmun Kirk consists of the Kilmun Arboretum and Forest Plots where many unusual foreign trees are under trial and are open to the public.

The road now runs through the village of Sandbank, where there are famous yacht-building yards. On approaching the main road ahead (halt sign) turn right to follow the upper reaches of the Holy Loch. Go on across the flat and fertile haugh lands of Dalilongart Farm, and bear right (signposted "Glasgow") at the first bend. The left-hand road leads to Glen Lean and the extensive woods on the Ballochyle Estate.

DIVERSION TO MASSAN (10 miles return)

Half-a-mile on, at the first bend, turn left on to a by-road signposted "Glen Massan" and "No through road", for a remarkable scenic run up Glen Massan. This public road plunges at once into the Sitka spruce plantations of the Ballochyle Estate managed by the Economic Forestry Group. Suddenly it skirts a deep bend of the swift River Echaig, where in summer salmon and sea-trout may often be seen leaping as they come up from the sea.

The road now winds past a group of the Forestry Commission's timber-built forest workers houses and skirts the grounds of Benmore House, now an outdoor educational centre. On the right, past the Golden Gates, close beside the Younger Botanic Gardens there will soon be seen, towering high above the roadway, magnificent trees including enormous Sitka spruces, Douglas firs, Noble firs from British Columbia, redwoods from California, and Monkey-puzzle trees from Chile. Most were planted about 1875 by Mr. James Duncan, who then owned Benmore Estate.

Now the road begins a steady winding climb up Glen Massan, through birchwoods that have been retained as a scenic attraction. On the left rise the plantations of the Ballochyle Estate and to the right those of the Forestry Commission. At a steepish bend where cars can be parked, you will find the Falls of Massan. Go down a short rocky slope towards the roar of their rushing waters, to see the remarkable cataracts that have scooped deep potholes and even a natural rock-arch, in the hard rocks of their bed. A good spot for a picnic, a paddle, or even, on a hot summer's day, a swim.

The public road continues for half-a-mile beyond the falls to Stonefield before becoming a private road leading almost to the head of Glen Massan. This is a wild and desolate tract of high sheep grazings, hemmed in by the steep crags of Creag Tharsuinn, or the "Oblique Rock-face", 2,103 feet high. Benmore—Beinn Mhor, the Great Hill, 2,413 feet—rises to the right of the road, and may be reached by a steep, three-mile, climb from the road-head.

The return must, of course, be made by the same route. Turn left on regaining the main road for the rest of our route.

MAIN ROUTE CONTINUES

Follow the main road to the bridge over the River Echaig. Once across, turn right (signposted "Strone"). Half-a-mile along, you will see on the left the modern District Office buildings of the Forestry Commission. Beside these, a car park has been provided for people wishing to visit the Kilmun Aboretum, described on page 110.

Just beyond these offices you will see, again on the left, Kilmun Kirk, behind which stands the ancestral burial vault of the Dukes of Argyll. The shores of the Holy Loch are now seen on the right, as the road skirts the peninsula south-east towards Strone Point. Beyond Kilmun Pier the main road hugs the shore. From the Point itself there are fine views over four great arms of the sea.

Looking south across the Holy Loch, which you have now encircled, almost completely, along three shores, you see Hunter's Quay, with Kirn near Dunoon beyond. The broadening waters of the lower Firth of Clyde reach out beyond it, right to the horizon, with the Ayrshire hills on the left, the Isles of Cumbrae ahead, and the Isle of Bute seen distantly as part of the right-hand coastline.

Eastwards, the upper Firth of Clyde runs up beyond Gourock Pier and the shipyards of Greenock and Port Glasgow, on the right-hand shore. The left-hand bank, looking up the Clyde, is the peninsula of Rosneath, with the townships of Cove and Kilcreggan hugging its shore. Helensburgh, beyond the mouth of the Gareloch, is hidden from view, but you can see the Kilsyth Hills rising just behind it, and perhaps, on a clear day, the breast-shaped mounds of Dumbarton Rock.

DIVERSION TO HILLSIDE VIEWPOINT (3 miles extra, round trip)

All that is needed to make this outlook still more spectacular is a vantage point above sea level. To gain this, follow the shore road for a mile north and then, just before Blairmore Pier, take a left-hand turn, climb a steep brae and bear left again. This leads back towards the Point, but 150 feet higher up. Halt as you approach Strone Castle, a Victorian extravaganza in the Scots baronial style. Take in the glorious panorama to the south and east. Then turn northwards for a view of the great Highland peaks, plainly in view above Loch Lomond. You stand here on the very edge of the great divide between Highland and Lowland Scotland.

MAIN ROUTE RESUMED

The original road (if you have in fact left it) is regained by a left turn at the hill foot. Follow it along the shore, now running up Loch Long, past the seaside villas of Blairmore. As you round Gairletter Point you will see this amazing fjord reaching far up into the Highlands between the steep flanks of its neighbouring hills. In the distance you are pretty sure to spot a huge tanker on its way to discharge oil at Finnart on the east shore—oil that will be pumped forty miles across Scotland to the Grangemouth refineries. The woods seen directly across the loch form part of the young Garelochhead Forest.

On the nearer shore, the spruces and hemlocks of the Glenfinart section of Benmore Forest come close to the road. Soon you reach Ardentinny, once a farming and fishing village with a ferry across Loch Long, but today a thriving settlement of forestry workers, retired persons and the modern Outdoor Pursuits Centre owned by Strathclyde Education Committee.

If time allows, visit the fine sandy beach or take a stroll towards the Shepherd's Point on Finart Bay or along the Forest roads.

Beyond Ardentinny the road, now winding, narrow and needing care, climbs steeply up the long Larach Pass to a height of 533 feet, with tall woods of spruce and larch on either side. It then falls, shortly and steeply, to Whistlefield Inn on Loch Eck-side. Here, take a sharp left turn on to the main road, A815. This leads directly back to Dunoon, twelve miles distant, and is clearly signposted throughout. See Route 2, following, but remember you are taking it in the reverse direction.

A couple of miles from Whistlefield, it is worth while to stop to see if you can descry a remarkable rock formation on the flank of Clach Bheinn. Looking up the glen of Coirantee, in Gaelic Coire an t'Sith or Corrie of the Fairy, you will see a huge kneeling, human figure. The modern name for this is the Praying Bishop, for imagination readily reads into its outline the cope and mitre of a high church dignitary kneeling before his prayer stool. To the pagan Gael, seeing it two thousand years ago, it must have suggested a giant or magic figure out of another world.

77

ROUTE 2. DUNOON TO BENMORE—LOCH ECK, GLEN-
BRANTER, STRACHUR, ST. CATHERINES,
CAIRNDOW AND ARROCHAR
(47 miles)

From Dunoon pier-head proceed up the main Street, Argyll
Street, north, leaving the town by a gentle climb to Loch Loskin,
embowered in surrounding trees. Descend to Sandbank and follow
signs saying "Glasgow" to the bridge across the River Echaig.

You are now in Benmore Forest, and its groves of spruce, larch,
sequoia, Douglas fir and hemlock sweep down to the roadside from
the steep hills on your right. To the left, the River Echaig winds
across a flat strath, past farm fields and shelterbelts. Approximately
a mile further on, you will come to a car park on your right hand
side. There you will find a board with a map showing way-marked
walks of varying lengths and destinations. These walks take you up
to Puck's Glen which is a fascinating rock chasm, with its waterfalls,
ferns, mosses and fine mature conifer trees. An access route through
the lodge gates, for pedestrians only, leads to the west shore of Loch
Eck; while on the opposite side of the road are more way-marked
walks, some of which link with Puck's Glen.

The road now climbs slightly, and the whole expanse of lovely
Loch Eck comes suddenly into view on the left. For the next six
miles the road hugs the shores of this freshwater loch, which is never
more than a quarter of a mile broad. The main features on the
farther side are the rounded mass of Clach Bheinn, the deep glen
called Coire an t'Sith, and the high massif of Beinn Mhor itself.
Following this comes the Bernice Gap, through which a track once
ran—from a ferry across the loch, to Glendaruel, Loch Fyne and
on by a further ferry towards Lochgilphead. Beyond Bernice runs
the ridge of Beinn Bheag, the Lesser Hill, and all the way the lochside is fringed with plantations of various ages.

On the eastern, right-hand, side of the road there are several
breaks in the plantations of the Loch Eck and Benmore sections of
Glenbranter Forest. First come the fields of Inverchapel, then the
Coylet Hotel and its paddocks, and next the Whistlefield Inn.
Behind this inn, the Larach road climbs steeply to the right, to wind
over the hill to Ardentinny on Loch Long. Two very fine clumps of
Scots pine grow by the loch shore here. A few groups of cottages
follow, and then the road reaches the level fields that border the
main river flowing *into* Loch Eck. This bears a different name to the
Echaig River that *leaves* the loch, six miles back. It is called the Cur,
and the district is called Strachur after its fertile, four-mile strath.

The first hamlet encountered is Glenbranter, named after a long
forested glen to the left. The Glenbranter Estate was once owned by

Sir Harry Lauder, who built the memorial to his wife and his son—who was killed in the First World War, that may be seen to the right of the highway (car park by A.A. box). His mansion, Glenbranter House, has been demolished, and on its site stands a new village, mainly of Swedish timber houses, in which live a busy group of forestry and timber workers. Near the bridge once stood the Mill of Driep, a watermill that ground all the corn grown in the district. Mary, Queen of Scots, slept at Driep during her tour of the Highlands.

The road now by-passes the old stone-built village or clachan of Strachur, and drops steeply down to Strachur Bay, on the shores of Loch Fyne. Here turn right (the left turn runs down the loch side towards Tighnabruaich), and follow the southern shore of Loch Fyne north-east towards Saint Catherines. Strachur House, near the road junction, will attract attention as a fine example of an early Scottish mansion. Loch Fyne, which is very deep, is rich in sea-fish, and you may quite likely see the accompanying fishers—a herring drifter, a flight of terns or "sea swallows", or even the dark head of a seal bobbing above the waters. From St. Catherines you can plainly see, across its two-mile width, the town and castle of Inveraray, the ancient seat of the Duke of Argyll. A ferry formerly plied here, but is now discontinued. The huge mountain seen far beyond is Ben Cruachan (3,689 feet), which is fifteen miles away on the shores of Loch Etive in Appin.

The road follows the loch shore to St. Catherines, and then climbs steadily, crossing moorland pastures where sheep graze right to the roadside. Three miles on you reach the turning (signposted, see Route 3 following) for Hell's Glen and Lochgoilhead. A halt here will repay you with remarkable views both south-west down Loch Fyne towards Inveraray and north-east towards the head of the loch and the great peaks beyond.

A curious feature will be found just through the field gate on the Loch Fyne side of the junction—a heart is marked on an old round surface by white stones set into the tarmac. This is the traditional wedding place for all the "tinkers" or gypsies who still wander through Argyll.

Our main route takes the *right-hand* turn and runs straight up Glen Kinglas, with steeply-sloping sheep grazings on either hand. At the first major bend, three miles on, it re-enters the Forest Park, and you can see on the left the Butterbridge Sitka spruce plantations of Ardgartan Forest. Butterbridge is the point where the women of the glens traded kegs of butter—one of the few marketable products of their crofts—for transport east by pack horse and boat. Ahead rise the "Arrochar Alps", the Park's highest and steepest hills, which culminate in Beinn Ime, 3,316 feet. On the right you see Loch Restil, with just beyond it a second branch road for Lochgoilhead (see Route 3 following).

You now emerge at the summit of the Rest-and-be-Thankful Pass, and follow the fine new road which sweeps down into Glen Croe, first through sheep pastures and then through great expanses of spruce woods on both hillsides. The old road, built early in the eighteenth century by Highland regiments as part of the measures taken to pacify the country, and repaired by that great road-maker General Wade, may be seen following its tortuous course down on the right; it is still used occasionally for hill-climbing trials. The two great hills opposite the modern road are Ben Donich, or Brown Hill, 2,777 feet, and The Brack or Dappled Hill, 2,583 feet.

After a winding four-mile descent the road reaches the flat lands of Ardgartan, on the shores of Loch Long. The River Croe, which we have followed downhill, has formed a delta jutting out into the salt water, and this hard gravelly promontory has proved ideal as the Park's main camping and caravan site. Other turnings to the right lead to the Ardgartan Youth Hostel, to the site run by the Camping Club of Great Britain and Ireland, and to sites reserved for young people's associations.

There is now a two mile run below the steep slopes of The Cobbler, to the head of Loch Long, where Glen Loin comes in from the north. Half-a-mile on, and you reach Arrochar, with its hotels, pier and major road junction. Before you leave it, halt to look across Loch Long to what is without doubt the most dramatic view in this region of magnificent landscapes. The broad summit of the mountain opposite is split into two separate rocky peaks with precipitous edges, and it is easy to see why the Gaels called it *An Goblach*, the Forked One. This has been corrupted to its colloquial English name of "The Cobbler", while Ben Arthur, its alternative Gaelic name, is rendered on the Ordnance Maps as "Arthur's Seat". This hill, which reaches 2,891 feet, is the principal climbing ground of the Park, as described in John Nimlin's chapter on the mountains. Beinn Narnain, the prominent mountain mass to the right, reaches higher, to 3,006 feet, and so just ranks as a "Munro", or named peak exceeding 3,000 feet in altitude.

ROUTE 3. ARROCHAR TO LOCH GOIL, HELL'S GLEN AND
CARRICK

For the first eight miles this route can be regarded as the end of Route 2, in reverse. From Arrochar, you drive round the head of Loch Long and follow the steady ascent of the Inveraray main road up Glen Croe to the head of the Rest-and-be-Thankful Pass.

At the top, turn left, on to a side road (single track, with passing places), signposted "Lochgoilhead". This first climbs a little higher. There follows a long descent down the curved slopes of Gleann Mor, the Great Glen, with the spruce woods of Ardgartan (Loch Goil) Forest to the left, and open hill grazings on the right. If you halt where the road crosses the burn (lay-by available) you may pick out the faint outline of a deserted crofting settlement. Above a sheep-fank, or stone-built shelter, there can be seen the ruined foundations of cottages, the ridge-and-furrow of the old lazy-beds where oats and potatoes were grown, and one or two of the rowan trees that were always planted as a shield against witchcraft.

The narrow, flat, flood-plain of the River Goil is reached at the hill foot. Continue on down the strath for three miles to Lochgoilhead village. This is a delightful, though isolated spot, completely encircled by hills and forests; its modest but historic pre-Reformation Church of the Three Brethren merits a visit. Loch Goil, which is six miles long and never more than half-a-mile wide, bends so much that its distant outlet cannot be seen. Its name means the "fork" or "branch", of the greater Loch Long, as the map aptly shows.

There are shops and a post office at Lochgoilhead, and also a camp and caravan site. The public road on the near, eastern bank, goes only for one mile before reaching Ardgartan Forest again, with only paths thereafter. The by-road on the farther, eastern shore offers an attractive scenic drive of five miles before it ends at Carrick Castle, now in ruins but once a stronghold of the Duke of Argyll. You can enter the ground floor of this roofless castle which stands on a rock jutting into the loch, and see also the narrow waterside entrance that people coming by boat could enter, even if the castle were beseiged on the landward side.

Leaving Lochgoilhead, the entry route is retraced for three miles. Then turn left for Hell's Glen, a narrow defile shut in by high crags rising on either side. The steep climb leads, after three miles, to the main Strachur–Arrochar route, just described as part of Route 2. Turn right to go back to Arrochar, or left if you wish to head for Strachur and Dunoon.

ROUTE 4. ARROCHAR DOWN LOCH LONG TOWARDS
GARELOCHHEAD, HELENSBURGH AND GLASGOW

This is a straightforward run down the side of Loch Long, following a road that needs care in driving owing to hills, bends, and an uneven surface. The westward views are magnificent and include in turn The Cobbler, Glen Croe, the Ardgartan plantations rising to the rugged heights of "Argyll's Bowling Green", and the meeting point of Loch Goil and Loch Long. Thereafter the road crosses a low divide to reach the Gareloch, which is followed into Helensburgh. Thence the road runs close to the Clyde's shore, through Dumbarton to Glasgow.

ROUTE 5. ARROCHAR TO TARBET, THENCE DOWN LOCH LOMOND-SIDE TOWARDS LUSS, DUMBARTON AND GLASGOW

Another easily-found route. Go east past Arrochar Station to Tarbet, turn right, and then follow Loch Lomond's western bank by the only available road. This is a better, though equally scenic, route south. The road, though level, winds continually through twelve miles of woodlands fringing Loch Lomond's shore, past Luss to Balloch. Even when traffic is light, high speeds are out of the question. There are splendid views of Ben Lomond, 3,192 feet, which lies across the loch in the Queen Elizabeth Forest Park.

Loch Long at Ardentinny

From this mountain's edge, clouds crowd
Where the path rises into absence.
Grass, and a few flowers I have not seen before
Stand out on the sky.

Moss also, clings to the stones, against the wind
That will not let up. A stream falls beside me
Feeding what still lives, deepening too fast
For thought to dare resist.

—Paul Mills.

WALKING ROUTES

By A. G. Bramwell

There are a variety of walking routes within the Park, ranging from short waymarked routes to long distance hill routes of which some but not all may be waymarked with coloured discs on a post. All of the Forestry Commission roads are open to the public on foot, but vehicles are not permitted. These roads enable one to reach the depths of the Forest, but many of them come to a dead-end with the result that one returns along the same route. Nevertheless they often enable one to reach a high level on a gentle incline up the side of a glen or hillside with the result that many fine views of the surrounding countryside can be obtained.

The weather can change rapidly in the mountainous area of the Park and walkers are strongly advised to wear stout footwear and be prepared for the onset of mist or rain. Anyone setting out on a hill route is advised to carry a map and compass and to inform a friend or his hotel or boarding house where he may be staying, of the route of his walk and the time at which he plans to return. Walkers in the Forest Park are asked to keep all gates closed, to take their litter home, to take care with matches and cigarettes particularly during the dry spring period and to keep their dogs under close control at all times—particularly during May and June when the young deer are born and the sheep are lambing.

The following is a description of some of the main walking routes within the Forest Park and which are indicated on the map in the folder at the back of this Guide. It is advisable to bear in mind that not all of the routes are circular, so you may need to arrange for a friend to meet you at the other end if you do not wish to retrace your steps.

NORTHERN AREA

Although just outside the Park boundary, Loch Sloy is well worth visiting. From Arrochar, a by-road goes up the east side of Glen Loin to Stronafyne Farm. A pleasant road continues for another mile or so to where a path ascends up to a low bealach and winds down to the croft of Coiregrogain. Here one joins the Hydro-electric Board road to the dam at the south end of Loch Sloy. A walk along the rampart of the dam provides a magnificent view of the Park area. Continue now by rough path along the west side of Loch Sloy. Half a mile before reaching the north end of the loch, bear west for one quarter of a mile and pick up another Hydro-electric road which leads down to Butterbridge on the Inveraray road. (Arrochar to Butterbridge by this route—11 miles.) Walk to the top of Rest-and-be-Thankful, returning to Arrochar by bus, or by the "old" road on foot. There is an alternative return route by the Hydro-electric road which leads to Glen Uaine, then over the bealach between Ben Ime and Ben Vane back to Coiregrogain and Glen Loin.

From Coiregrogain also one can go by road up Allt Coiregrogain to the road end under Ben Ime. From here it is but a mile to the Bealach a'Mhaim, a flattish area surrounded by Ben Ime, The Cobbler and Ben Narnain. The choice lies now between the upper waters of River Croe to Glen Croe or by the lochan at the head of the Buttermilk Burn and down that burn to Arrochar. In mist it is easy to lose one's way at the Bealach and a compass is required.

An alternative route to Coiregrogain is by the forest road on west side of Glen Loin. This road starts about half a mile up the glen beyond Succoth Farm. It winds south at first, then near the head of Loch Long it turns north and finishes near the end of the Hydro-electric road, by which a return can be made.

It is now possible to go from Arrochar by "forestry" and "old" roads to the top of Rest-and-be-Thankful, avoiding altogether the crowded and dangerous main road. One starts at the head of Loch Long and goes by road up the west side of Glen Loin for half a mile. Thence a new forestry road winds back south along the hillside, crosses the Buttermilk Burn and winds up and then down to the main road in Glen Croe. One can now either use the old "Rest" road to the summit or cross the River Croe at Craighdhu and take a forestry road which winds high up through woods to finish near the Lochgoilhead road.

CENTRAL AREA

A maze of forestry roads here form a paradise for the walker, as cars are not allowed over them. One must, however, keep to roads till above forest level. There are endless possibilities as roads seem to go off in all directions. Suggestions would be from Ardgartan Forest Office by Coilessan Glen road. This goes to head of the glen, then climbs high and circles round to finish in a dead end above Loch Long. Return by same route from Ardgartan by Mark road, past the Camping Club of Great Britain site to the first road. Fork on right (Cat Craig road) which winds over the hill to Glen Croe at Creaghdhu, returning to Ardgartan by the Creagdhu road (about 5 miles). Mark, Guanan Beag and Dail roads and back by Mark road (8 miles). To deserted cottage of Mark, by Mark road, returning as above (13 miles). It is not advisable to try and return from Mark by lochside. Though the distance between Mark and Feolian road-end is only about two miles, the going is incredibly difficult. Corran Lochan road branches off west from the Mark road and its end, almost twelve miles from Ardgartan Forest Office, is the southern end of the road system. It finishes above Corran House (NS/210939) and is a highly scenic route throughout its length.

ABOVE THE FORESTS

The finest hill walk in the whole area is by way of the ridge of hills in the centre of the Ardgoil peninsula. Give a whole day to this. It is a lovely route to be taken leisurely. From Ardgartan Forest Office go by forest roads down the west side of Loch Long to Corran Lochan, a lakelet in the hills. Now turn north and climb The Saddle (1,704 feet). The route is obvious now; go steadily north gaining height at each successive peak, over Beinn Reithe (2,141 feet) and on to Cnoc Coinnich (2,497 feet); then make a descent to the bealach and a final climb to summit of The Brack (2,580 feet). This peak has dangerous cliffs on its north face, hence descend north-west to the bealach between The Brack and Ben Donich and follow indicated route through plantations to the forestry road at Creaghdhu. The hill walking is easy throughout, but if too long one can omit The Brack and descend by Coilessan Glen to Ardgartan.

A "NON-PATH"—A WARNING TO VISITORS

From time to time adventurous folk have tried to walk from Lochgoilhead to Ardgartan via the shore-side. Often they have failed and have had to be taken off by boat. There is no path whatever round the ultimate part of the peninsula. Often the rock falls sheer to the lochside and the ground is complicated with trees, deep heather, bracken and brambles—brambles like barbed wire. That route is not recommended and it should be noted that the House of Corran has no communication by road or path—only by boat.

Another scenic road starts half a mile south of Craigbrack and goes along the hill-side parallel with the main road and above Whistlefield Inn, finally to join the Glen Finart road.

LOCHGOILHEAD TO ARDGARTAN

There is a choice of three routes to Ardgartan, the two shorter ones being each about 6 miles in length and the longer route, via the Corran Lochan, about 12 miles. Of the shorter routes, the Glen Croe path is a gradual uphill climb and a steep drop into Ardgartan, while the route via Coilessan Glen involves a steepish climb up to the head of the glen and a downhill descent to Ardgartan. All three routes begin in Lochgoilhead where cars can be parked in the village square beside the Post Office. The start of the walks is about 200 metres up the side road leading from the square, past the village shop.

GLEN CROE ROUTE (6 miles)
Waymarking—White discs

Follow the white markers up through the forest to where the path joins a rough track running up the south side of the Donich Water. Cross the burn by the footbridge and continue up the valley to a point where the path bears left handed. From here, look back down across Loch Goil to Beinn Tharsuinn (2,307 feet). Follow the path up the side of the Alt Coire Odhair between Ben Donich (2,774 feet) and The Brack (2,580 feet) to a point where the path begins to descend to the burnside. From here a fine view can be seen back down the glen and across to the Lettermay Valley where the steep waterfall flows out of the Curra Lochain down into the Lettermay burn and divides Ben Lochain (2,306 feet) from its neighbour Ben Bheula (2,557 feet). As you cross the burn, notice the pile of stones on your left. This is probably the remains of a shieling, a temporary dwelling which was used by the crofters when grazing their stock on the high slopes in the summer.

Just beyond this point the path crosses a series of humps or moraines; deposits of clay, sand and boulders left behind by a glacier during the last ice age. As you round the shoulder of Ben Donich into Glen Croe it is worth leaving the path slightly to cross to the very large boulder on your right, from where there is a magnificent uninterrupted view of Glen Croe with Long Long just visible at the bottom of the glen. At the head of the glen is the Rest-and-be-Thankful Pass, at the foot of the rocky slopes of Beinn an Lochain (2,992 feet). Directly across the glen is The Cobbler (2,891 feet) and looking down the glen over Loch Long the high ridged peak of Ben Lomond (3,192 feet) can be seen on a clear day. Return to the path and follow it down through Ardgartan Forest to the Forest Office where cars may be parked across the burn from the office.

COILESSAN GLEN ROUTE
Waymarking—Blue discs

Take the previous route to the point where the path divides and from here follow the *Blue* markers up the side of the hill to the saddle between Cnoc Coinnich (2,497 feet) and The Brack (2,580 feet). From here you can look back down over Lochgoilhead and ahead to Ben Lomond, the high sharply ridged peak of which will be obvious on a clear day. Cross to the head of the Coilessan Glen, looking down to Loch Long and across to Glen Douglas opposite, which runs through to Loch Lomond. Follow the path down the burn side to the forest road and hence to Ardgartan Forest Office.

These two routes can be combined into one expedition, beginning and ending at Ardgartan and making a circuit of The Brack. Distance 10 miles.

CORRAN LOCHAN ROUTE (12 miles)
Waymarking—Yellow discs

This route has the same starting point as the previous two. Follow the *Yellow* discs along the forest road and up behind Lochgoilhead. The road continues along the face of Beinn Reithe (2,141 feet) with some fine views down and across Loch Goil. Leave the road just above Stuckbeg and follow the burn up between Beinn

Reithe and The Saddle (1,704 feet) and through the small area of natural birchwood on to the open hill again. Follow the path round to the edge of the Corran Lochan to the forest road. Before turning back down the road it is worth going south up the forest road a little way to look down Loch Long towards the Clyde estuary. Return to the path which follows the forest road down Loch Long. Just after leaving the Lochan it is possible to look down over Loch Long to the Gareloch and its junction with the Clyde just north of the town of Greenock. The path ends at the Ardgartan Forest Office where cars may be parked across the burn from the office.

LOCHGOILHEAD TO GLENBRANTER (7 miles)
Waymarking—Orange discs

Park your car in the village and follow the road for 1½ miles south of Lochgoilhead on the west side of the loch to Lettermay farm. The route starts here and follows the forest road up the valley of the Lettermay Burn to a point where the road ends and a path continues up through the plantation on the face of Cruach nam Miseag (Hillock of the She-Goats). On leaving the forest the path skirts round the edge of Lochan nam Cnaimh, a typical West Highland lochan and ascends to the saddle between Sgurr a Choinnich (2,148 feet) and Beinn Bheula (2,556 feet). From the crest of the saddle a fine view can be had back down the Lettermay valley to the distant wooded slopes of Beinn Lochain (2,306 feet), Beinn Tharsuinn (2,037 feet) and Ben Donich (2,777 feet). Follow the path round the face of Sgurr a' Choinnich and down to the Coire Ealt burn. Follow the burn down to a point just above the forest edge where one can look down over the top of Loch Eck to Bheinn Beag (2,029 feet) with Glenbranter running behind it. The path leaves the open hill here and follows the forest road down through part of Glenbranter Forest to the A815 at a point 1 mile above the head of Loch Eck. Limited car parking is available at this point.

LOCHGOILHEAD TO STRACHUR (7 miles)
Waymarking—Red discs

Follow the previous route to Lettermay Farm. A little way up the forest road the route divides. Follow the markers down to and across the Lettermay burn from where the path climbs the face of Beinn Lochain (2,306 feet) round to a point between Ben Bheula (2,556 feet) and Beinn Lochain. From here one can look down across the Lettermay Glen to Cruach nam Miseag (1,989 feet). Follow the path along the edge of the burn to the Curra Lochain, which is about 1,050 feet above sea level. The path continues along the northern bank of the lochan, through Bealach an Lochain (The

Plate 58. Sunlight on the Hat Pool, a well-known spot for salmon on the Echaig close to Benmore.

Plate 59. Glenbranter Forest clothes the hills above the fields and village in the glen.

Plate 60. Pony trekkers high on the slopes of The Cobbler above Ardgartan.

Plate 61. Forest roads make ideal riding routes on a sunny day.

Plate 62. The North Peak summit of The Cobbler.

Plate 63. An amazing winter prospect from The Cobbler's summit. Looking east over Loch Long (*hidden*) the Tarbet Gap (*right*) and Loch Lomond to Ben Lomond's snow-capped summit. The scene embraces two Forest Parks—Argyll this side of Loch Lomond and Queen Elizabeth beyond.

Plate 64. A rambler on The Cobbler's north peak gazes southwards over the south peak towards Glen Croe (*hidden*). The rugged Brack rises beyond.

Plate 65. To a skilled mountaineer, glissading offers an exciting means of descent. Well-equipped winter climbers start a glissade from a point near The Cobbler's north peak.

Plate 66. The main road from Arrochar towards Inveraray climbs up Glen Croe towards the Rest-and-be-thankful Pass. The Cobbler's south peak towers above Ardgartan Forest. These woods are scarred by a great wind-blow, since replanted. A forest office and a tourist information centre lie on the left.

Plate 67. The new Youth Hostel at Ardgartan on the shores of Loch Long.

Plate 68. At the pier-head, Dunoon.

Plate 69.   A view north up Loch Fyne from a point near St. Catherine's, on the road that links the north and south portions of the Park.

Plate 70.   Dunderave Castle, an ancient stronghold of the Campbells, built in the rugged Scots baronial style, on the north shore of Loch Fyne.

Gap of the Lochan) and down the Leavanin Burn between the wooded slopes of Carnach Mor (2,079 feet) and the open sheep ground of Cruach Nan Globa (1,848 feet). Cross the burn at the forest edge and, closing the gate behind you, follow the forest road round the heavily wooded slopes of Beinn Lagan (1,526 feet) to Strachurmore.

These two routes can be made into one excursion from Glenbranter to Strachur. The approximate distance is 13 miles.

ROUND BEINN LAGAN

A delightful walk all by forest roads. From a point midway between Strachur and Glenbranter village, the Succothmore road goes up the north side of the River Cur. The Beinn Lagan road starts at Strachurmore Farm and goes up the south side of the river and winds right round the hill to descend at Invernoaden near the Lauder Monument. (Strachur to Strachur, 10 miles.)

VIEWPOINT ROAD

Possibly the most scenic road of all starts just south of the Lauder Monument following the *Orange* discs route and winds high up almost to limit of the forest, finishing some way south of Coire Ealt. At several places it gives magnificent vistas right down Loch Eck. If keeping to the road, one must return by the same way. From Coire Ealt, Beinn Bheula (2,557 feet) is within easy reach.

SOUTHERN AREA

ARDENTINNY TO CARRICK CASTLE

A comparatively easy low level walk with no steep climbs and approximately half the length being on a forest road.

Leave your car at the park opposite Glenfinart Beach near the Forestry Commission Office and follow the forest road which starts from behind the office.

Keep bearing right wherever a road junction occurs and you will find yourself walking along the shores of Loch Long for about 3½ miles. You will have the chance of seeing a number of eider duck and a variety of sea birds, in addition perhaps to a submarine exercising in the loch or an oil tanker en route to the pipeline terminal on the opposite shore of the loch at Finnart.

The route then passes under a major power line and you leave the road for a path through the plantation which eventually emerges on the edge of agricultural land and the southern shore of Loch Goil.

Having followed along the shore the route joins the public road to Carrick Castle, where a welcome refreshment can be obtained in the hotel.

During your walk you may pass within sight of campers. These will be either Scout groups or groups from the three Adventure Centres located within the Park, who have specific permission to use these sites for periodic camping as part of their training.

ARDENTINNY TO STRONCHULLIN FARM AND GAIRLETTER POINT

This is an easy route following a forest road throughout.

Leave your car at the public car park in the centre of Ardentinny village and follow the path leading towards the forest boundary and into the forest itself. You will then shortly join a forest road, where you turn left. At the first junction you come to on this road you have the choice of going straight ahead on a low level route to Stronchullin farm or bearing right on the high level route to the farm. In this latter case, bear left at the next junction and straight on thereafter.

Both the routes pass through plantations of various ages and species and provide periodic views across to Loch Long and up to the head of the loch at Arrochar to the north, with the fine mountainous panorama in the background.

On leaving the plantations the routes merge in Stronchullin Farm fields from where one can obtain fine and extensive views of the surrounding landscape and across to the Firth of Clyde.

The route turns left at the end of the fields and passes through the Stronchullin farm yard before joining the Kilmun to Ardentinny road on the shore of Loch Long at Gairletter.

Having reached this point one can turn left to return to Ardentinny or link with the periodic bus service to the village.

GAIRLETTER TO BENMORE GARDENS OR PUCK'S GLEN

This is a fairly strenuous walk with part of the route being at a high level over the hill.

Leave your car on the shores of Loch Long just south of the Gairletter caravan site. Follow the forest road past the gravel quarry which supplies material for construction of the forest roads, and through the gate into the plantation. A small silver mine used to be in operation in this area about ninety years ago. Keep straight on up the glen at the first and second road junction until you come to the coloured marker which takes you up the hill and out of the plantation leading towards the pylon line. As you descend the other side of the hill you have fine views to the south overlooking Holy Loch and the Firth of Clyde with the mountains of the Isle of Arran in the distance. To the west lies Loch Eck beyond which in the far distance may be seen part of the Kintyre peninsula.

You will eventually re-enter a plantation where you join a way-marked forest trail and have the choice of either following the *Black* marker to the Benmore Gardens car park, or the *Red* marker leading down the picturesque Puck's Glen to the car park at the bottom of the glen. Both car parks are on the Dunoon to Loch Eck road. (For a description of these trails please see below.)

BENMORE GARDENS TO GLENBRANTER

A low-level walk on a forest road along the west side of Loch Eck with no steep climbs.

Leave your car at Benmore Gardens car park and enter the Gardens by the Black Gates at the Lodge and not by the side entrance for those paying to enter the Gardens. Cross over the River Echaig and turn right and right again at the next junction along the forest road to Bernice. The first stretch of the road is tarmaced as far as the site of the new water filtration plant constructed in 1975. Follow the road for its entire length along the tree-lined shore of Loch Eck. You will pass through both conifer plantations of various ages and species and through agricultural land grazed by hill sheep and cattle. The loch is a popular fishing area and the haunt of a variety of water birds. It is also used by pupils at the Benmore Adventure Centre for canoeing practice, while the rocky scarps and hills to your left are used for rock climbing practice and hill walking exercises.

At the northern end of your walk you will arrive at the Headquarters of Glenbranter Forest. Follow the tarmac road to your right and past the timber built forest worker houses and over the River Cur where you rejoin the Strachur to Dunoon road which runs along the eastern shore of Loch Eck.

FOREST TRAILS

These are circular waymarked routes of varying length through the Forest.

At Benmore Forest you can leave your car at either Benmore Gardens car park at the Black Gates or at Puck's Glen. Both are situated on the Dunoon to Strachur road about 5 miles from Dunoon and a diagramatic map sign at both parks helps you to choose your route.

A. Starting at Benmore Gardens Car Park —

The *Yellow* route is a short circular path of about 400 yards for those who require a brief walk before continuing their car or bus journey.

The *Brown* route is a walk of about 1 mile. After a gradual climb up, amongst the fine mature specimen trees of Douglas fir, Noble fir, redwood and Western red cedar planted in 1880, you pass through younger plantations planted in 1952 before turning right down the hill until you reach the old public road. Turn right when you reach this road and it is a short distance back to the car park.

The *Red route* is a fairly strenuous but very picturesque walk of about 3 miles ending at Puck's Glen car park, or totalling about 4 miles if you return on the circular route to Benmore Gardens.

Having left the first part of the *Brown* route described above, you pass through a variety of young plantations on a gradual uphill gradient. After about $\frac{3}{4}$ of a mile you can either continue straight on to the top of Puck's Glen or turn right and still follow the *Red* marker along a forest road, past a viewpoint of the surrounding countryside until you reach the middle of Puck's Glen itself. From here you can either follow down the glen or continue on to Kilmun Arboretum and the car park at the Forestry Commission Office.

If, however, you have decided to carry on to the top of the glen (where you link with the hill walking route to Gairletter on the shore of Loch Long—see page 90) the route then starts descending alongside the burn with fine conifer trees of many different species and ages on either side. (See notes on the *Black* route for a brief description of this same route in reverse.)

Eventually you reach the bottom of the glen at the car park. If you turn right and follow the old council road you arrive back at Benmore Gardens after about 1 mile.

B. Starting at Puck's Glen Car Park —

The *Black* route is a fairly strenuous but picturesque walk of about 3 miles ending at Benmore Gardens car park, or totalling about 4 miles if you continue on the circular route back to Puck's Glen car park. A short way up the glen you can, however, return on a shorter circular route (*Red* route) to the same car park.

The *Black* route is in fact the *Red* route described above, but in reverse.

The first part is a gradual climb through a variety of mature conifer trees towards the glen itself. Many of the fine trees planted in the glen in 1880 by James Duncan, one of the original owners of Benmore House and Estate, were blown down in the hurricane of 1968. The burn at the foot of the glen was blocked in many places with the result that the original bridges and dry stone wall abutments to the path were washed away. The path has been restored by the Forestry Commission with valuable help from volunteers of the Conservation Corps in Scotland.

As you walk up the glen you will find a wide variety of mosses, liverworts and ferns which thrive in the moist atmosphere. In addition you will see a variety of seedlings and older trees that have seeded themselves from the many fine specimens of mature conifer trees that survived the hurricane. These include the Sitka and Norway spruce, Douglas fir, Western red cedar, Western hemlock, Scots pine, European larch, redwood and Noble fir.

Half way up the glen you will come to a forest road where you have the option to continue to the top of the glen or turn left along the road where you rejoin the *Black* route on its return to Benmore Gardens. A turn to the right on this road will take you to the Kilmun Arboretum and the car park at the Forestry Commission Office at the head of the Holy Loch.

If you decide to carry on to the top of the glen you link with the hill route over to Gairletter on Loch Long, or return on the *Black* route towards Benmore Gardens.

When you arrive at the car park at the entrance to the Gardens you have the option of returning to your departure point at Puck's Glen car park, by turning left and following the route of the old public road for about 1 mile.

Bless to me, O God,
The earth beneath my foot;
Bless to me, O God,
The path whereon I go;
Bless to me, O God,
The thing of my desire;
Thou Evermore of evermore,
Bless thou to me my rest.

—Am Beannachadh Turais: *The Journey Blessing*
(Traditional).

In their orange and pink anoraks the mountaineers
spider up the glass mountain; they suck glucose,
their crampons crunch into the snow of the cornice
and their ice-axes swing in their mittened hands.

Pitons and karabiners jangle at their waists;
the rope skips between them and the wind
snatches at the disturbed snow; soft snow
balls up between the spikes of their crampons.
                              —Tom Buchan, *The Mountaineers.*

MOUNTAINS OF THE PARK

By John Nimlin and Stan Tanner

THE highest mountains in the Park form a compact group at its
northern end. Ben Ime (3,318 feet), Ben Narnain (3,036 feet),
A'Chrois (2,785 feet) and Ben Arthur (The Cobbler) (2,891 feet)
are the four main summits, but Ben Vane (3,004 feet), Ben Vorlich
(3,092 feet) and Ben an Lochain (2,985 feet) are outliers of the same
group, although not within the boundaries of the Park.

The four peaks within the Park attract an increasing number of
climbers, both for their crags and gullies which interest the rock and
snow specialists, and for their fine situation amid some of the best

scenery in the West Highlands. It is with this latter virtue that we are concerned, and the opportunities it offers to the mountain tramper in quest of new scenes and interesting experience. The details of rock and snow climbing features are beyond the scope of this article.

Arrochar is the best centre for exploration, lying as it does within a few hours' range of all the summits, besides offering accommodation to suit all tastes; youth hostels, camping grounds and hotels. Three of the mountains are within view of the village. To the south is The Cobbler, with the striking profile which makes it the most popular peak in the district. In the centre is the rocky gable-end of Ben Narnain's south-east ridge which hides the actual summit, and to the north, linked to Ben Narnain by the high ridge of Creag Tarsuinn, is the smaller peak of A'Chrois. Ben Ime lies out of sight beyond them.

THE COBBLER

The path to The Cobbler starts from the lay-by at the Succoth road end (NN/294050), rises through the forest, crossing a series of stiles until it reaches the hydro-electric water tract. Bearing west across the lower slopes of Ben Narnain, the path reaches the Allt a' Bhalachain (Buttermilk Burn) level with the small dam. Another path starts a few paces west of the Allt a' Bhalachain where it flows under the new road above the Torpedo Testing Station (NN/287042) and climbs up its left bank to join the first path near the 1,250 feet contour. From this point, there is a choice of tracks on either bank of the burn and they are followed for about a mile on slowly rising ground to the 1,750 feet contour, where the burn from the Cobbler Corrie joins the Allt a' Bhalachain. This smaller burn is then followed at a steeper angle into the corrie, which is a wide, crag-enclosed hollow bounded on left and right respectively by the cliffs of the South and North Peaks, with the less precipitous Centre Peak in the middle.

At close range the crags are imposing. Walls of silver-grey rock are folded and squeezed in places into great breaks which overhang their bases. In bad weather when the mist eddies around the corrie, the place is wild and forbidding, but one fleeting ray of sunlight will transform the light-hued rocks and the mountain vegetation into a scene of life and colour.

On either side of the Centre Peak, there are breaches in the crags comprising steep grass and scree slopes which give the best routes to the summit ridge. From the ridge, easy slopes lead up either side of the Centre Peak which is the highest point on The Cobbler. The summit of the North Peak is also within easy reach of the ridge though the going can be slippery and dangerous in wet weather, but the South Peak, with crags on all sides, is best left to experienced rock climbers.

The view from the summit is very extensive. It commands Ailsa Craig, Arran and the Clyde estuary to the south, the peaks of Jura, Mull and Ben Cruachan to the west, and covers a great expanse of mountains to north and east, ending in the haze-filled depression of industrial Clydesdale. The view from the other peaks in the area is essentially the same, with some difference in the foreground. A'Chrois, for instance, has its own special view of Loch Lomond; Ben Narnain has the wild recesses of Coire Sugach under its eastern face, and Ben Ime has views into Glen Kinglas and Coiregrogain Glen.

A suggested line for the descent would be the long south-east ridge pointing to Loch Long. A little track passes behind the summit rocks, and curves round the Glen Croe side of the South Peak to the broad grassy ridge, which is followed along the crest and then descended in a southerly direction to Ardgartan, or by its north-east slopes to the Allt a' Bhalachain and the two converging tracks mentioned for the ascent.

BEN NARNAIN

The first part of the route to Ben Narnain takes the same line, but it keeps to the right of the Allt a' Bhalachain until two large boulders are reached near the 1,500 feet contour. The lower one overhangs on one side, and a wall of turf and stones has been erected against it to make a rough shelter for four or five persons. It is the resort of week-end climbers who prefer to bivouac without a tent, and it is estimated that it has from 150 to 200 bed nights in a year. Its vicinity is also much used by mountain campers. The other boulder, well known as the Narnain Stone, provides many little rock-climbing problems, its surface being scored by the nail marks of climbers' boots.

From the boulders a small burn is followed up the south slopes of Ben Narnain into a shallow, crag-fringed corrie which gives a fairly steep scramble to the ridge. The route then goes north along the base of the square-cut "Spearhead" ridge to the flat, stony summit. There is a south-east ridge on Ben Narnain, similar to the one on The Cobbler, and although its sides are steep and craggy, its crest gives a good line of descent. At the end of the ridge where it over-looks Loch Long, a few zig-zags may be required to avoid rocks, but once below them, easy slopes will be found all the way to the path from the Succoth road end. Yet another route is suggested by the high ridge between Ben Narnain and A'Chrois. This ridge may be followed to A'Chrois without any great loss of height, and the excursion gives fine views of Ben Ime, Ben Vane and Coire Sugach.

A'CHROIS

From Ben Narnain, A'Chrois is merely seen as the termination of the high ridge, but in the views from upper Glen Loin and Coiregrogain it appears as a well defined peak with many of the features of a true mountain. Supporting the summit to the east there is a fair stretch of crag with a shapely corrie below it; this is a favourite resort of snow climbers. The simplest approach from Arrochar is by the track on the right side of the Sugach Burn, followed by a traverse across the lower end of Coire Sugach to the grassy southern slopes, which offer no obstacles to the summit. This would also make a good descent to the round traverse from Ben Narnain. Coire Sugach is also well worth a visit, for its rugged scenery, its mountain plants, and its air of seclusion, and it entails a relatively easy climb for an off-day.

BEN IME

The route to Ben Ime, which is the highest mountain in the district, is similar in its first stage to the routes given for The Cobbler and Ben Narnain. The Allt a' Bhalachain route is again taken, but this time there is no divergence from the course of the stream. It is followed up the glen between The Cobbler and Ben Narnain to the watershed, which is crossed and descended a little to the cairn marking the crest of the pass between Coiregrogain Glen and Glen Croe. Beyond the cairn and in a northerly direction, long grass slopes are climbed with the eastern escarpment falling away to the right hand. A few hundred feet from the summit the route then takes a sharp leftward bend to avoid the steep northern corrie, and beyond this, easy slopes lead to the bulky cairn which is a feature of Ben Ime. For the descent a route could be taken down the course of the Croe Water between Ben Luibhean and The Cobbler to the main road in Glen Croe, or a return could be made to the cairn on the pass, where a descent to the east would land one in Coiregrogain Glen. This glen would then be followed to the catchment dam, where a forest road bears east and then south along the lower slopes of A'Chrois to bring one out above the head of Loch Long. For climbers who prefer hill-passes to peaks, this cairn on the pass is the central point. A route could follow the Allt a' Bhalachain over the cairn, then turn east down the Allt Coiregrogain or west down the Croe Water, or a direct crossing could be made between Coiregrogain Glen and Glen Croe.

After a few visits to the district it will be seen that many other routes and variations are possible.

As a complete traverse of all four peaks can be done in one day it will be clear that the single ascents are well within the powers of an average climber, but allowance must be made for bad weather. Mist or snow can transform easy places into dangerous ones. The rocky outcrops which give the ruggedness to the Arrochar hills are dangerous pitfalls in mist or driving snow, and at all seasons a compass and a one-inch map should be carried. If lost in the mist it is possible to follow most of the main streams down to the glens, provided great care is taken. Although this may mean a long weary grind to the starting point, it is better than a damp night on a hillside.

The vast perspectives distance, the lost lands,
Innocent, green, where dark corrodes
With the sea, mind and jaw to one purpose,
Action that will not claim its end.

—Paul Mills.

THE NAMES
The hills wear their Gaelic names like old-fashioned hats. Is Meall
Dubh no more than a Black Lump? What will happen to a
language when it survives only in the names of hills, like the
ancient pines in ones and twos, the remains of enveloping forests?
—Robin Fulton.

GAELIC PLACE NAMES

Translations by
J. M. Bannerman and William L. Inglis

A'CHROIS	The Cross
A'CHRUACH	The Hill
ALLT COIR-GROGAIN	The Burn of the Twisted Corrie
AM BINNEIN	The Summit
ARDENTINNY	*Ard*, height; *an*, of; *teine*, fire—Hill of fire, of *Bel*, *Belus*, or *Baal*—The sun god
ARDGOIL	*Ard-a-ghobhail*—Height above the Fork of the two Lochs—Long and Goil
ARDNADAM or ARNADAM	*Ard*, *aird*, height; *na*, of the; *damh*, *daimh*, oxen—Hill of Oxen
ARGYLL (Argyle)	*Ar*, land; *gaidheal*, Gael—Land of the Gael (the stranger or foreigner)
ARGYLL'S BOWLING GREEN (Monachriggan)	This is a playful name for the range of mountains occupying the peninsula of Cowal northward from the junction of Loch Goil and Loch Long. Within the compass of the area the principal peaks are Clach Bheinn (1,433 feet); Tom Molach (1,210 feet); The Saddle (1,704

99

feet); and Bheinn Reithe (2,141 feet). The range was in the pathway of the early cattle drovers on their way to the markets of the south, and here the Duke of Argyll's men rested their cattle for the night. The Gaelic name for the pass was *Argyll's Buaile—an grian* (Argyll's sunny cattle fold). Due to carelessness in printing or translating the area on the earlier ordnance survey map was over-printed "Argyll's Bowling Green". Monachriggan is "The Rocky Mountains"

ARROCHAR	*Ard*, high; *tir*, land—The high country
BALLOCHYLE	*Bealach*, a pass; *al, ail*, beautiful—The lovely pass
BALLYGOWAN	*Baile*, town; *gobhainn*, smith—Town or village of the smith
BARNACUBBER	*Bearn a Cobhair*—Gap of refuge
BEACH	*Bid*, a summit
BEALACH AN LOCHAIN	The gap of the lochans
BEALACH A MHAIM	The opening on the ridge
BEINN AN ARMUINN	Peak of the Chief
BEINN BHEITHE	Peak of the Birches
BEINN BHEAG	Little Peak
BEINN BHREAC	Mottled Peak
BEINN DONICH	Brown Peak
BEINN DUBHAIN	Peak of the Black Burn
BEINN IME	Peak of the Butter Making
BEINN LAGAIN	Peak of the Inlet-Bay
BEINN LOCHAIN	Peak of the Lochans
BEINN MHOR	*Mhor*, great; *beinn*, hill or ben—The great hill (2,433 feet)
BEINN NAN LUIBHEAN	Peak of the Herbs
BEINN RUADH	*Beinn*, hill; *ruadh*, red—The red hill or hill of red deer
BEINN TARSUINN	Oblique Peak
BEN ARTHUR	Arthur's Peak, or possibly "Peak of the Great Bear" (Welsh *arth awr*) from its shape
BENMORE	*Beinn mor*—The great hill. Ancient name, Innis-nan-rusg—Sheltered vale of the fleece. This is the highest hill in the Dunoon district, but it is almost flat on top, with good grazing
BEN VANE	The White Peak

BERNICE (Hill and Glen)	*Beur*, a pinnacle; *nan eas*, waterfalls—The pinnacle of the waterfalls
BERRYBURN (Burn of the Berry)	*Bar, barra*, point—Burn of sea point
BLAIRMORE	*Blair, blar*, battlefield; *mhor*, great—The great battlefield
CARN GLAS	The Grey Cairn
CARNACH MOR	The Big Rocky Mass
CARRAIG NAN RON	The Rock of the Seals
CARRICK	*Carraig*—Rock
CLACH BHEINN	Stone of the Mountain
CLACHAIG	*Clachach*, stony; *ach*, full—The stony place
CLADYHOUSE (now Sandbank)	Clyde house, *Clyda, Clady;* or *Cladach*, stony beach—House of the stony beach
CLOCH	*Clach*—Stone
CNAP REAMHAR	The Broad Mass
CNOC A'MHADAIDH	The Wolf's Hillock
CNOC COINNICH	Hillock of the Foxes
CNOC NA TRI-CHRICHE	Hillock of Three Boundaries
COBBLER (Ben Arthur)	The *Beinn copach*—The jagged hill, or *Beinn gobhlach*—The forked hill
COILESSAN	*Coill-easan*—The Wood of the Waterfalls
COLINTRAIVE	*Caol-an-t-snaimh*—Creek or swimming narrows. In the olden days cattle from Bute were made to swim across to the mainland
CORLARACH HILL (near Bull Rock)	*Corr*, round pit; cup-like hollow; *learach*, larch trees—Round hill of the larch
CORRAN	Sickle-shaped Bay
CORRAN LOCHAN	The Lochan by the Sickle-shaped Bay
CLYDE	*Cli*, strong; *ad*, water—The strong stream or water. Hence *Clutha, Clyde*, and *Clady* (Erse). It would appear that this name is derived from a river goddess meaning the washer or the strongly flowing one
COTHOUSE	*Coite*, punt or small boat; *tigheadas*, household The small house of the boat; the punthouse.
COWAL (*Gobhal* or *gabhal*)	A fork-prong; land between the lochs, glens and streams; enclosed land. Dr. Skene asserts that Cowal takes its name from Comgall, one of the two grandsons of Fergus. The old name was *Comgaill*
COYLETT	*Caoi*, way; *caol*, narrow; *leth*, side—The narrow part (the narrowest part of Loch Eck)
CREACHAN	Hard bare rock

CREACHAN BEAG	Little Hill
CREACHAN MOR	Big Hill
CREAG DUBH	Black Rock
CREAG MHOLACH	Bare Rock
CREAG TARSUINN	Oblique Rock
CRUACH A 'CHAISE	Hillock of Cheese Making
CRUACH AN DRAGHAIR	Ridge Hillock
CRUACH BHUIDHE	Yellow Hillock
CRUACH EIGHEACH	Hillock of the Shouting
CRUACH NAN MISEAG	Hillock of the She-goats
CUR	*Ur, eur, oir*, water; *curr*, heron
CURRA LOCHAIN	Marsh of the Lochan
DUNOON	*Dun, on*—The little hill or fort. Buchanan calls it *Norum Dunumm vel Dunum in Coralia*, the new fort. Dr. Jamieson said: "Dunoon is generally pronounced in aspirated form —*Dunan*, and another derivation is *Dun*, a hill, fort, or castle, and *Nuin*, the Irish Gaelic for ash tree. The vicinity of the castle, church, and village was covered at one time with such trees, and one great ash grew in Argyll Street near or on the site of the Clydesdale Bank. One other meaning —*Dun*, a fort; *obhainn*, a stream, a river"
ECHAIG or EACHAIG	*Ech, ach*, water; *Eck, Oich*, Loch Eck— The Eck water or stream. Some of the names in *ag* are from the names of animals, such as *eoch*, a horse.
ECK	*Ach, uch, uach*, water, high—The upper water. *Oice, oich*
FINNART	From *fionn*, white and *ard*, a headland— White headland
FINART GLEN	Dale of the Finart
FINARTMORE	*Fan, faoin*, slope; *ard*, high; *mhor*, great— The great steep slope
FINARTEBEG	*Beag*, small—The small slope
FYNE (Glen or Loch)	*Fyne*, middle; The middle glen
GAIRLETTER	*Garbh*, rough; *leitir*, side—Rough eastern side of Blairmore Hill
GANTOCKS	*Caonteach*, water spirits or kelpies haunting rivers
GARELOCH	*Gearr*, short—the short loch
GLENBRANTER	*Gleann*, dale; *bran*, black, poor; *tir*, land— Dale of poor land or soil

GLENCROE	*Cro*, sheep cot—Glen of sheep cot
GLENDARUEL	*Gleann*, dale; *ruadhail*, red; *ruel*—Dale of red water or blood. Old name, Glen of dark water
GLEN LOIN	Glen of the Pool or Rivulet
GLEN MASSON	*Gleann*, vale; *Masson*, long hill or stream (also spelt *Massan*)
GLEANN MOR	Big Glen
GLEN SHELLISH	*Glen seileach*—Glen of Willows
GLEN STRIVEN	*Stroibh*, strife—The vale of strife
GLEN TARSAN	*Tar-suinn*, across, oblique—The oblique glen
GOIL (Loch)	*Goil*, sulky, boiling, raging or: the fork
GOUROCK	*Noc*, knoll; *geard*, rough—Rough knoll. Could be from *Guireoc*, rounded hillocks
GREENOCK	*Gren, grean*, from *Grian*, the sun; *cnoc*, knoll—Knoll of the sun; or *Grianach*, sunny place
HOLY LOCH	*Loch Seanta* or *Seunta*—The charmed loch. *Loch Naomha* or *Loch Naomh*—Holy Loch
HUNTER'S QUAY	Called after Mr. Hunter, of Hafton, who built a pier at *Cammusreinach* (old name), meaning Fern Bay)
INNELLAN	*Inne*, little; *ailleann*, a fair green sward—The little meadow. Others say Island of Birds (The Perch)
INNIS-NA-RUSG	Old name for Benmore—*Innis*, sheltered vale; *na rusg*, fleece—Cosy vale of the fleece
INVERARAY	*Inbhir*, confluence, bed; *aray*—Bend of the River Aray, the water of worship
INVERECK	*Inbhir*, confluence, cove, or creek; *ach, eck*, water—Cove or creek of the Eck River.
INVERCHAPEL	*Inbhir*, cove or *inbhear*, pasture; *capull*, horse—Horse pasture, or bay of loch
KILCREGGAN	*Cill*, a cell; *a*, of; *Mhuna*—Instruction place or cell of Saint Mun (St. Munde)
KIRN	*Carn*, heap of stones; or *cearn, churn*, corner or nook—The stone quarry; the nook. The harvest home (Scots)
KNAP	(Pronounced "crap".) A steep hillock
KNOCKAMILLIE (Innellan)	*Cnoc*, a hill or hillock; *milidh*, soldier; *mealaich*, broom—Knoll of warrior (ruins of old castle), or broom knoll
KNOCKDOW	*Cnoc*, hill or hillock; *dubh*, black—The black knoll, or the black hill

KYLES	*Cuil*, corner; *caolas*, the straits—The corner of the straits between the Isle of Bute and the mainland of Argyll
LAIGH	Low lying land
LARGS	*Learg*, plain—The fields
LARACH HILL	*Learach*, larch trees; or *larach*, field of battle— Hill of the larch trees or hill of battle
LETTERMAY	*Leitir Mhaighe*—Sloping Plain
LOCH GOIL	*Goil*, sulky, boiling, raging—The stormy water
LOCH GILP	Water of the Gilp
LOCH LONG	*Loch*, arm of the sea; *loin*, low water or channel—Loch of the little water or ship loch. Once called *Naves longae*—Bay of Ships
LOCH RESTIL	*Loch ros teile*—Loch of the Point of Lime Trees
Mark	Pasture-land for horses
MASSAN	*Mas*, a long hill; *an*, water; *Massan*, glen of the long hill (Ben Mhor). Also claimed to be a personal name—Massan's Glen
MEALL AN T-SITH	Fairy Mound
MEALL BREAC	Speckled Mound
MEALL DARAICH	Oak Mound
MEALL DUBH	Black Mound
MEALL REAMHAR	Thick Mound
MORAG'S GLEN	*Gleann*, dale; *muirioc*, seaside; *moruach*, mermaid; *Muire-oig*, Virgin (Mary); *oig*, pure —Glen of Mermaid or Mary. Known at one time as Malcolm's Glen
MUN or MUNDE	The abbot of abbots. *Fintan Munna* of Ireland, who founded Kilmun in the beginning of the 7th century. The only Columban or Culdee Church in Scotland
OTTER	*Oitir*, a sand bank—Ridge of the sea
RASHFIELD	Is simply a translation of the old name, *Achluachrach*, the field of rushes
ROSENEATH	*Rhos neoth*, bare promontory; or *ros-na-choich* Peak of the Virgin or of little dingle
RUDHA NAN EUN or RUDHA AN EOIN	Promontory of the Birds
SANDBANK	Named after the sandy shore at the head of the Holy Loch. Old name, *Cladyhouse*
SGURR A'CHANNAICH	Peak of Bog-cotton
SLIGRACHAN HILL	*Slighe*, a path; *gragan* or *creagan*, rocky— The hill of the rocky path

SRON CRICHE	The Boundary Point
ST. CATHERINE'S	*Cairine, Ceit, Caitriana*, Saint—Ruins of Saint Catherine's Chapel
STRATHECHAIG	*Strath Echaig*—Valley of the Echaig. Old names, Strathcachie, Stratheghy
STRACHUR	*Strath*, valley; *ur*, water. *Cur*, heron—Valley of the heron. Old name—*Kilmaglass*—Burying ground of (Saint) Maglass
STRIVEN (Loch)	*Stroibh*, strife—The loch of strife. Ancient name, *Caolan*, narrow—The narrow loch
STRONAFYNE	Headland of Fion or Fingal (symbolical—a virtue)
STRONE	*Sron*, a nose, point. The end of the ridge
STRON SAUL	*Sron*, promontory; *sal*, great—The great promontory
STRONCHULLIN	*Sron*, point; *cuillean*, little wood; *cuillion*, holly—Promontory of little wood or holly grove
STUC	A Peak
STUC-BEAG	Little Peak
SUCCOTH	*Sugach*—Point of land jutting out between two rivers
TARBERT	*Tairbeart*, isthmus; *tara*, to draw—The narrow neck of land across which boats are drawn from one water to another
TARSAN (Glen)	Dale; *tarsuinn*, cross, across—The oblique glen
TOM BUIC	Hillock of the Roebuck
TOM MOLACH	Tufty Hillock
TOM NAN GAMHNA	Stirks Hillock
TOWARD	*Dubh* (doo) black, dark; *ard*, height—The black height. Old name—Tollart
WHISTLEFIELD	*Tigh-na-feed*—The House of the Whistle. Old wayside tavern called Whistlefield from habit of travellers blowing a whistle when wanting a ferry from the far side of a loch

105

With winter on this island
we sense the beat of spring
when brisk Atlantic rollers—
broken first on skerries
of the outer isles—
make foam and spume
along the cliffs and caves
while tufts of sea-thrift
wait the winter out.

—Charles Senior.

GENERAL INFORMATION

THE information given here is to assist you in planning your visit to the Park whether it is to be short or long. It is not claimed to be the last word for the situation is always changing. The sources are quoted to enable the visitor to check the up-to-date situation.

TOURIST BOARDS

The Scottish Tourist Board, 23 Ravelston Terrace, Edinburgh 1, supplies excellent information covering the whole of Scotland which will enable you to plan your holiday to include a visit to this and other Forest Parks. They will also provide the addresses of local tourist associations.

Dunoon and Cowal Tourist Organisation, Pier Esplanade, Dunoon, Argyll, covers the whole of the Park and maintains an

Information Office at Creag Dhu on the A83 road some 4½ miles west of Arrochar. This organisation produces an accommodation list and supplies attractive brochures for all the major recreational facilities.

MAPS

Ordnance Survey 1: 50,000: Sheet 56 covers the greater part of the Park and to this should be added Sheet 63 for the southern tip.

Ordnance Survey one-quarter-inch-to-the-mile, Sheet 6 Firth of Clyde, is a useful guide for motor touring.

See also the folding maps in the pocket of this Guide.

ACCESS TO THE PARK

Since the previous edition of the Guide was published much of the local public transport service has been withdrawn and the situation may change during the currency of this edition. For descriptive purposes Dunoon and Arrochar are taken as the main gateways to the Park.

AIRPORTS
Glasgow

Glasgow Airport, Abbotsinch, Paisley, distant some 17 miles from Gourock and 30 miles from Arrochar.

RAIL SERVICES

Nearest rail accesses to the area are at Gourock (Ferry to Dunoon 20 minutes) and Arrochar on the north-eastern boundary. From Balloch pier Caledonian MacBrayne Ltd. also operate the *Maid of the Loch* steamer service on Loch Lomond during the summer. This trip provides distant views of the northern end of the Park and of the Queen Elizabeth Forest Park to the east.

At Stirling British Rail have a Motorail Terminus for cars from the south.

BUS SERVICES

Western SMT Co. Ltd. operate four outward and inward services daily from Anderston Cross Bus Station, Glasgow to Arrochar and beyond along the A83. Details: Phone 041–221–1924.

This service gives access to the northern end of the Park.

In the south, A. Baird Ltd of Dunoon run service buses from Dunoon to Ardentinny and also to Strachur. Details: Phone Dunoon 2088.

Coach and self-drive car hire facilities are available in Dunoon and Arrochar. Details from Tourist Information Centres.

The Caledonian MacBrayne Company operates half-hourly, large boat services for vehicles between Gourock and Dunoon. Western Ferries run similar services, with smaller craft, between Cloch Point (1 mile west of Gourock) and Hunter's Quay (1 mile north of Dunoon. Details from Tourist Information Centres or Motoring Organisations.

Access routes for walkers and cyclists are not listed as they generally prefer to determine their own routes from the maps available. The chapter in the Guide "Seeing the Park by Road" gives valuable guidance to motorists.

NOTE: VEHICLES, EXCEPT THOSE AUTHORISED FOR FORESTRY OR FARMING, ARE NOT PERMITTED ON FOREST ROADS.

ACCOMMODATION

The most useful general information is to be obtained from the Guide Book and Accommodation Lists of the Dunoon and Cowal Tourist Organisation and the usual Guides produced by motoring and other associations. Hotels, Bed and Breakfast Houses, restaurants, Cafes, Inns and Bars are well distributed throughout the areas. The local Tourist Organisation also lists details of Caravan Parks and other self-catering holiday accommodation.

Centres under which accommodation in Cowal is listed include

Dunoon, Sandbank, Kilmun, Strone and Ardentinny, Loch Eck and Strachur, Lochgoilhead and Carrick and Cairndow.

The Clyde Tourist Association office at Tarbet, Loch Lomond, covers accommodation in Arrochar.

CAMPING AND CARAVAN SITES

There are numerous sites around the Park area which are listed in the usual Guides. Within the Forest Park the Forestry Commission offers the following facilities:

Ardgartan Caravan Site

A beautiful site at the head of Loch Long with access to the loch and to walking in the adjoining forest. This site has a resident warden who welcomes and assists the visitor. Services are up to the highest standard and shopping facilities are provided.

Details of the charges, which vary from time to time, are shown in the pamphlet, Forestry Commission Camping and Caravan Sites, post free from the District Office, Forestry Commission, Kilmun, Argyll. As a guide, the rates in 1975 were 32p per person per night; children aged 5–15, 16p; subject to VAT.

Youth Camp Sites

On a minimum facility basis the Forestry Commission also provide a series of Youth Camp Sites scattered throughout the Forest Park. Some are for the sole use of the local Outdoor Centres but bookings for the facilities near Arrochar can be made in advance by written application to the District Forest Office, Forestry Commission, Kilmun, Argyll.

NOTE: NO CAMPING OR OVERNIGHT PARKING IS PERMITTED WITHIN THE PARK OTHER THAN AT THE ABOVE SITES.

YOUTH HOSTELS

The only Scottish Youth Hostel Association accommodation is at Ardgartan near Arrochar on the shores of Loch Long. This hostel is well situated for climbing expeditions or boating as well as providing a base for all the varied recreational activities of the Park. Bookings and enquiries from the Warden (Arrochar 362).

OUTDOOR RECREATION

ANGLING

In addition to the fresh water lochs and rivers the Park area is bounded by the sea lochs of the Clyde basin which is among the foremost of the sea angling areas of the British Isles.

A. *Forestry Commission Facilities.* 1975 prices. Season April-September.
River Finnart, Ardentinny. Sea trout and the occasional salmon.
Permits from either Angle Cottage, Ardentinny, Dunoon; or
The Forester, Forestry Commission Office, Glenfinart, Arden-
tinny, Dunoon (Ardentinny 253).
50p, plus VAT, per day.
River Goil, Lochgoilhead. Sea trout, salmon and brown trout
(5 rods per day limit).
Permits from Chief Forester, Ardgartan Forest Office, Forestry
Commission, by Arrochar, Dunbartonshire (Arrochar 243).
£1.10, including VAT, daily.
Lettermay Burn, Lochgoilhead. Sea trout and brown trout.
Permits from Chief Forester, Ardgartan Forest.
27p, including VAT, per day.
Lochan nan Cnaimh, Lochgoilhead. Brown trout.
Permits from Chief Forester, Ardgartan Forest.
Ardyne Burn, Toward. Sea trout (4 rods per day).
Permits from Mr D. Crawford, Forestry Commission Ranger,
Linhemohr, Toward, Dunoon.

B. *Other Facilities*

In addition to these Forestry Commission facilities in the Park
there are many more in the Cowal area.
Full details can be obtained from the Tourist Information
Centre (Dunoon 3755).

SEA WATER ANGLING

This sport is expanding and boat hirers multiplying so rapidly
that no attempt is made to give a list. Suffice it to say that apart
from the unlimited opportunities for fishing from the sea shore if
anglers are prepared to walk, boat hire facilities are available at
Dunoon, Kirn, Sandbank, Ardentinny and Arrochar.

CRUISES

Cruises on the Clyde and the sea lochs afford splendid views of
the Park. Details from the Tourist Information Service (Dunoon
telephone 3755).

GARDENS

Kilmun Arboretum

The main entrance to this interesting and varied collection of
trees from all over the world, is from the car park at the Forestry

Commission's District Office at Kilmun. The entrance is clearly signed off the A880 Dunoon to Kilmun and Ardentinny road.

An illustrated guide book is available at the Forestry Commission's Office and the Tourist Information Office, in Dunoon (*Kilmun Arboretum and Forest Plots;* HMSO, Edinburgh; 10p).

The Arboretum is very well worth a visit from both the family party and the amateur or professional botanist and forester. All the various species are clearly labelled with their name and country of origin and the area is divided into sections by waymarked footpaths which can be easily followed with or without the assistance of the guide books. The highlight of a visit to the area is probably to see the fine collection of "gum trees" or *Eucalyptus* species. They are all growing at a very fast rate and their picturesque foliage and bark, together with the fragrant smell in warm weather, can at times give one the impression of being in a semi-tropical country.

In addition, the route of the paths climbing up the hill, produces excellent views of the surrounding countryside and of the Holy Loch.

Younger Botanic Garden, Benmore

The Department of Agriculture and Fisheries for Scotland maintain the Younger Botanic Garden at Benmore on the A815 from Dunoon–Strachur, which holds an unrivalled collection of rhododendrons and is a delightful place to visit at all times of the year.

SAILING

For the experienced yachtsman Loch Long and Loch Goil in the heart of the Park give excellent opportunities for sailing. Dinghies are available on hire from the Chalet and Watersport Centre at Carrick Castle, Lochgoilhead (Lochgoilhead 249).

Sailing tuition can be obtained from Clyde Sailing Holidays, "Netherfield", Sandbank (Sandbank 245).

A regular series of races are held by the Holy Loch Sailing Club and Toward Sailing Club, who welcome visitors wishing to take up membership. Visitors should ascertain addresses of Hon. Secretaries from the Tourist Information Centre.

ORIENTEERING

The rugged terrain of the Park offers many interesting opportunities for orienteers to practice their skill and prestigious competitions are becoming more frequent. Details may be obtained from the Hon. Secretary, Scottish Orienteering Association, "Bernhill", Pitcorthie Road, Dunfermline, Fife.

GOLF; BOWLING GREENS; TENNIS COURTS

Facilities are available as follows:

Golf at Cowal Golf Club, Dunoon (18 holes);
Innellan Golf Club (9 holes);
Strone Golf Club (9 holes).

Bowling Greens are available in Innellan, Dunoon, Kirn and Sandbank.

Tennis Courts are available in Dunoon and Innellan.

SHOOTING

A. *Forestry Commission Facilities*

Day permits for deer stalking and grouse shooting in season may be arranged by contacting the Conservation Forester, Silver Fir Cottage, Taynuilt, Argyll (Taynuilt 613).

B. *Clay Pigeon Shooting*

The Cowal and District Gun Club hold events at Kilmun. Enquiries should be addressed to the Secretary, Mr. A. Thomson, "Cumbrae View", Innellan, Argyll (Innellan 268).

SWIMMING AND SUB-AQUA

There is a well equipped swimming pool on Alexandra Parade, Dunoon. Bathing is permitted in most of the fresh water lochs, though the visitor is advised to enquire locally for the best and safest places.

The Chalet and Watersport Centre, Carrick Castle, Lochgoilhead (Lochgoilhead 249) have wet suits and compressed air for hire.

The Dunoon Sub-Aqua Club meet in the Swimming Pool on Sundays and welcome visitors. Air for hire.

WALKING

See chapter on Walking Routes.

PHOTOGRAPHY

The opportunities for photographic studies are unlimited. The Cowal Camera Club, Castle Street, Dunoon, shows exhibits from time to time during the summer.

NOTE: WILD LIFE PHOTOGRAPHY IS NOT PERMITTED WITHIN THE FOREST PARK WITHOUT A FORESTRY COMMISSION PERMIT.

PONY TREKKING

Organised trekking holidays, schooling and day rides are available at The Riding School, Lochgoilhead, Argyll. Enquiries should be addressed to Mr. Douglas Campbell, Lochgoil Caravan Park, Lochgoilhead, Argyll (Lochgoilhead 312).

PICNIC SITES

On the shores of Loch Eck on the A815 from Dunoon to Strachur three picnic sites have been created each with limited car parking facilities. The sites are located at Rubha Garbh, Rubha Croise and Dornoch Point (see Map).

On the B828 road from Rest-and-be-Thankful to Lochgoil there is a very attractive small picnic site on the banks of the Glean Mhor burn at MR 53/206063.

Further Forestry Commission picnic sites will be established during the currency of this edition and notified to the Tourist Office.

NOTE: PLEASE USE THE LITTER BASKETS OR TAKE YOUR LITTER HOME AND LEAVE THE SITE AS YOU WOULD WISH TO FIND IT.

SPECIAL FACILITIES

These may be arranged within the Forest Park, through the District Office, Forestry Commission, Kilmun, by Dunoon, Argyll (Kilmun 422). Examples of such facilities are:

Sponsored Walks and other similar events, *School and Group Visits, Specialist Study* requirements, etc.

Car Rallies may be attended by contacting the Secretary, Royal Scottish Automobile Club, 11 Blythswood Square, Glasgow G2 4AG (041–221–3850).

THE LASS O' ARRANTEENIE

Far lane amang the Hielan' hills,
  Midst nature's wildest grandeur,
By rocky dens, an' woody glens,
  Wi' weary steps I wander.
The langsome way, the darksome day,
  The mountain mist sae rainy,
Are naught tae me when gaun tae thee,
  Sweet lass o' Arranteenie.

Yon mossy rosebud doun the howe,
  Just op'ning fresh and bonny,
Blinks sweetly neath the hazel bough,
  An's scarcely seen by ony:
Sae, sweet amidst her native hills,
  Obscurely blooms my Jeanie—
Mair fair an' gay than rosy May,
  The flower o' Arranteenie.

—Robert Tannahill.

Arranteenie is a local name for Ardentinny.

Printed in Scotland for Her Majesty's Stationery Office by McCorquodale (Scotland) Ltd., Glasgow
Dd 132041/3475 K128 1/76